REFERENCE INTERVIEWS, QUESTIONS, AND MATERIALS

Third Edition

by
THOMAS P. SLAVENS

I.C.C. LIBRARY

The Scarecrow Press, Inc.
Metuchen, N.J., & London
1994

British Library Cataloguing-in-Publication data available

Library of Congress Cataloging-in-Publication Data

Reference interviews, questions, and materials / edited by Thomas P.
    Slavens. -- 3rd ed.
           p.   cm.
    Accompanied by: An Answer key to the third edition.
    ISBN 0-8108-2718-2
    1. Reference services (Libraries)--United States. 2. Reference
    books.   I. Slavens, Thomas P., 1928-
Z711.R4437   1994
025.5 ' 2 ' 0973--dc20   93-24488

To Cora

TABLE OF CONTENTS

PREFACE

The purpose of this book is to assist students in learning to locate information. It is based on the idea that the best way to learn to use reference works is to use them. It is intended for library and information science students in their first course in reference materials and for students in colleges and secondary schools for library orientation and bibliographical instruction programs.

The book is divided into chapters based on types of reference works: encyclopedias, yearbooks, statistical sources, biographical works, bibliographies and library science reference works, dictionaries, handbooks, serial publications, directories, and government publications. Within these chapters, three subdivisions are provided. The first of these subdivisions is labeled "Reference Interviews." These conversations are stenographically recorded interviews which have taken place in public, academic, school, and special libraries. Permission has been secured from the libraries involved to do this task, which required 700 hours to accomplish. At the same time, it is impossible to identify any patron or librarian involved in this project.

The reason for including these interviews is to give students some idea of the real world in which they will be working. None of the interviews has been created artificially. It would be useful for students to attempt to answer these questions to give them a sense of realistic questions, as well as to understand how such questions are frequently phrased and the degree of skill which is required to elicit from readers the exact nature of the information desired.

The second subdivision in each chapter is a list of questions which can be answered from basic reference sources. The reason for including these queries is the belief that the student wanting to know how to use reference materials can attend lectures and discussion groups on reference materials; but until they use the works to locate data, they do not understand fully the types of materials available to meet the informational needs of readers. A third subdivision in each chapter is a list of sources in online, CD/ROM, microform and print formats in which the answers to the questions may be located.

An answer key to all the questions in the book will be supplied to teachers requesting such a key, addressed to the publisher on official stationery. Every attempt will be made, however, to safeguard the security of these answers.

Each professor will have to determine how many of these questions are to be used. One of the reasons for including so many is that the questions can be divided among students, thus reducing the probabilities of collaboration in answering them--if a teacher finds this undesirable.

In short, then, this book is intended to be useful to students as they attempt to become acquainted with a wide spectrum of representative sources of information and to learn to use these in meeting the informational needs of readers. For library orientation programs, it is hoped that the book will be useful in acquainting students with the wide variety of reference materials available.

The cooperation of the people who participated in the preparation of the book is acknowledged, although this group is so large that it would be impossible to name them all.

Thomas P. Slavens
Professor of Information and Library Studies
The University of Michigan

CHAPTER 1

ENCYCLOPEDIAS

Reference Interviews

Patron #1. A woman caller

Patron: What can you tell me about New Britain, Connecticut?
Librarian: Do you want to know where it's located or what it contains?
Patron: I want information like what industries are there, and if there are any colleges or universities there.

              Where would you look?

Patron #2. A high school boy.

Patron: I was wondering if you could help me find a list of all the Roman emperors?
Librarian: Do you just want a list or some information on them?
Patron: Just a list.

              Where could a list be found?

Patron #3. A high school boy.

Patron: Do you have a history encyclopedia?
Librarian: What was it that you had in mind to look up?
Patron: I need a chapter on the Gold Rush.
Librarian: In the United States?
Patron: Yes.
Librarian: Do you know when it happened? There were several, I think.
Patron: The one I want was around 1848.

1

| Librarian: | Is there any other word we could use for Gold Rush? |
| Patron: | Sometimes they're called the Forty-Niners. |

Where would you find this information?

Patron #4.   An elementary school boy.

Patron:	We're studying maps. Where can I find information on them?
Librarian:	Are you studying history or kinds of maps or something else?
Patron:	Kinds of maps.
Librarian:	Did you want books, magazine articles, or encyclopedia articles?
Patron:	I just want something I can read here.

What would you suggest?

Patron #5.   A high school boy.

Patron:	Does the library have a pamphlet on fascism?
Librarian:	Are you doing a report for school?
Patron:	Yes.
Librarian:	Just fascism in general or some more specific aspect of it?
Patron:	Just in general.
Librarian:	Did you check the card catalog for a book?
Patron:	Yes, but I don't want to read a book.

Where could you find general information?

Patron #6.   A junior high school boy.

Patron:	We're studying languages in school. Where do I go to find out about them?
Librarian:	Do you have any special language in mind?
Patron:	Yes, I'm supposed to find out about pidgin English.

Where could you check?

Patron #7.   A man.

Patron: Do you have a picture of the Colossus of Rhodes?
Librarian: Is that one of the Seven Wonders of the World?
Patron: Yes. It was a statue but I think it's been torn down
                 now.

                 Where could sketches be found?

Patron #8.   An elementary school boy.

Patron: My teacher said to find out about this. (He hands the
                 reference librarian a note with the word "equus" printed
                 on it.)
Librarian: Do you know anything about this equus at all?
Patron: No.
Librarian: What are you studying in class?
Patron: Horses.
Librarian: Do you think maybe this is a kind of horse?
Patron: It could be.

                 Where would you find this information?

Patron #9.   A high school boy.

Patron: Where do I find information on the Ku Klux Klan? It's
                 not listed in the *Readers' Guide*.
Librarian: That seems odd. How are you spelling it?
Patron: Cu Cluck Clan.
Librarian: It's spelled with k's and the middle word is Klux.
Patron: Oh, I'll check again.
Librarian: Most of those articles are about recent events. Did you
                 want an historical look at the Klan; for instance, what
                 its role was following the Civil War?
Patron: Yes, that was my assignment.

                 Where would you locate this information?

Patron #10.   A student.

Patron: I want some information on meiosis.
Librarian: For which class is this?
Patron: Biology.
Librarian: Do you have to write a report?
Patron: Yes, and I want to make a chart.

                 Where would you look?

Patron #11.   An elementary school boy.

Patron: I need to find out all about Michigan's forests.
Librarian: Do you want to find out where they are located, how to
                 be a forester, or Michigan's forests as an industry?
Patron: I need to know about where they are and what kinds of
                 trees they have and stuff.

                 Where could you check first?

Patron #12.   An elementary school boy.

Patron: Do you have any books about costumes?
Librarian: Yes we do. Do you want a book on how to make
                 costumes or costumes of different countries and times?
Patron: Well, I really want pictures of army uniforms.
Librarian: Oh, I see. Do you want foreign army uniforms or
                 American ones?
Patron: Well, sort of. I have to do a project in school about the
                 Revolutionary War. We can do anything we want so I
                 thought I'd draw pictures of the different uniforms of
                 the Revolutionary War soldiers.

                 Where would you look for good illustrations?

Patron #13.   A man.

Patron: Say, I've got a problem. Do you know anything about
                 potatoes?
Librarian: What do you want to know about potatoes? How to
                 grow them? How to cook them?

Patron: Oh no, nothing like that. You see, a few guys at work
               have a bet going. One guy says that sweet potatoes and
               yams are the same thing, and the rest of us say that
               there's a difference. Can you find out for me?

               Where would you check?

Patron #14.   A high school boy.

Patron: Do you have any books about tobacco?
Librarian: We have several books on smoking and also botany
               books which would contain information on tobacco.
               What exactly are you looking for?
Patron: Well, I'm doing a paper on smoking and its history and
               I want to find out who discovered tobacco and where
               it's grown, how they make it into cigarettes and cigars
               and stuff like that.

               Where could you locate this information?

Patron #15.   A student.

Patron: I need some information about Iwo Jima, you know, the
               mountain where they put up the flag.
Librarian: Do you know the name of the mountain?
Patron: It is Mt. Suribachi.
Librarian: I don't see anything under Iwo Jima or Mt. Suribachi.
               The entry must be World War II.

               Where would you look?

Patron #16.   A student.

Patron: I need to find out about Christianity.
Librarian: Is this for history class?
Patron: Yes.
Librarian: That is a big subject. What phase of it do you need?
Patron: I don't know. Just general, I guess.

               Where could you find general information?

Patron #17.   A student.

Patron: I want some information on Gutenberg.
Librarian: Is this for your Bible class?
Patron: No, it is for English composition class.
Librarian: Do you need mostly information on the Gutenberg
                Bible or on Johann Gutenberg?
Patron: I have to give an oral report on some of the
                characteristics of Gutenberg; a character sketch.

                Where could this be found?

Patron #18.   A student.

Patron: I want to find a copy of the text of the 25th Amendment
                to the Constitution.

                Where would you check?

Patron #19.   A small girl.

Patron: Do you have any books about cows?
Librarian: What kind of book did you want? A picture book or a
                story book?
Patron: Well, I want to know if a cow has two stomachs or not.

                Where could this be answered?

Patron #20.   A student.

Patron: Do you have any books on the 13 colonies?
Librarian: We have a section of books on early American history.
Patron: I have a list of questions on who founded the colonies,
                etc.
Librarian: The *Oxford Companion to American History* gives
                names and dates of ratification.
Patron: I need more information than that. I have six questions
                on various things.

What would you suggest?

Reference Questions

1. Compare the bibliography for the article, "Acts of the Apostles" in the *Encyclopaedia Brittannica* and the *Encyclopedia Americana*. Which has the longer article?

2. Compare closely the biographical detail given in the *Encyclopaedia Brittannica* and the *Encyclopedia Americana* for Louis Agassiz, 1807-1873.

3. What is the meaning of "Aijeleth Shahar"?

4. Compare the anatomical illustrations in *Encyclopedia Americana* and *Grand Larousse* , e.g., eyes and muscles. Which are better?

5. Find a table showing the illegitimate children of Louis XIV.

6. What work by Aristophanes did Frank Kupka, 1871-1957, illustrate?

7. Find a portrait facsimile of Sir Richard Arkwright, famous British inventor.

8. Who was responsible for the posthumous publication and popularity of the writings of Gustavo Adolfo Bécquer? Was there an English translation before the 20th century?

9. Compare the entries on "Birds" in the *World Book* and Compton's. Which do you think is better?

10. Find a portrait of Nicholas Murray Butler (1962-1947).

11. Locate a brief sketch of Maria Callas.

12. Where would you find color illustrations of Carolingian art?

13.   Which has the better maps and illustrations for China, Compton's or *World Book*?

14.   Compare the costume illustrations of the *Grand Larousse* with those under "Clothing" in the *World Book*.

15.   Name some of the superior characteristics of hybrid corns over other varieties.

16.   Can you find a picture of the 14th Dalai Lama of Tibet?

17.   Wanted: pictures of some of the work by the famous sculptor Enrique Claraso y Daudi.

18.   Find an illustration of Jacques-Louis David's painting of Madame Récamier.

19.   Where is "S. Agnese" by Andrea del Sarto? Locate a reproduction.

20.   Find a map of the city of Dessau.

21.   Find an illustration of a bust of Titus Flavius Domitian, Roman emperor.

22.   Locate a brief illustrated sketch on ancient Egyptian funeral architecture.

23.   When and where is the Feast of Dolls celebrated?

24.   Find the music (13 bars) of the national hymn of Finland.

25.   What is the English translation of the refrain of the French national anthem?

26.   Locate a statement of Gadow's classification of birds which includes a list of the principal characteristics of each category.

27.   Find articles on Alexandre Gendebien.

28.   Wanted: an article in English which will give one a scholarly, historical treatment of genealogy.

29.   To which encyclopedia would you go for a disposition of the opposing forces at Gettysburg, and to which for a clear plan of the battle area, and to which for illustrations?

30.   Where is the Gogebic Range located?

31.   When was gold first discovered in California, and by whom?

32.   Where may be found a reproduction in color of a page from the 42-line Bible?

33.   Find a table showing the changes—name and territorial—made in the states of India since 1947.

34.   Find a list of notable persons, with dates, whose homes were or are in Iowa—a list containing at least 25 names.

35.   Did Isyllus of Epidaurus dedicate a poem to Apollo of Malea?

36.   Who sculpted the Iwo Jima Memorial, Arlington, Virginia? When was it dedicated?

37.   What was the size of the army allowed to Jehoahaz by Hazael?

38.   Where and when was the composer Paul Juon born?

39.   Find a portrait and autograph facsimile of Johannes Kepler.

40.   Locate a color photo of limonite, an iron ore.

41.   Cite a brief historical sketch (15-20 lines) of Magdalene College, Cambridge University. What famous English politician bequeathed his library to the college?

42.   What is the Chinese game from which the popular 1920's game Mah Jong was adapted?

43.   Where was *Manon Lescaut* first staged and when?

44. What are some of the paintings and illustrations for which Frans Masereel is known?

45. Who was governor of Massachusetts in 1926?

46. What was the duration of the Ming dynasty in China?

47. Find a picture of Ann Jarvis, who suggested Mother's Day.

48. In which foreign encyclopedia can one find the best maps of Napoleon's campaigns?

49. Locate an illustration of Navajo sand painting.

50. Find a reproduction of the arms of the city of Pau.

51. Locate a short bibliography (partially annotated) of works since 1940 on perfumes and cosmetics.

52. Where is Iloilo?

53. What is the elevation of Rib Mountain? Is it a state park?

54. What was the Ribbon Society?

55. Find a signed article on the French painter Maurice Utrillo.

56. What was the "grass roots movement" and how was it connected with the writings of Fyodor Dostoevsky?

57. Locate a facsimile of the signature of Jean-Jacques Rousseau.

58. Find a plan of the church of Sancta Sophia in Constantinople.

59. Find a portrait of Scanderbeg.

60. Find an article on Albert Schweitzer in any of the encyclopedias.

61. Locate the plans of Seville cathedral and the coat of arms of Sheffield.

62.   Where is there a biographical sketch of G.B. Shaw which includes his photograph, his autograph, and a fairly complete list of works by and about him?

63.   Cite a monograph on the history of shorthand or stenography showing the alphabets of early British schemes (16th to 18th centuries) and of the Pitman and Gregg systems.

64.   Find a ground plan of Solomon's Temple, Jerusalem.

65.   What is the color of the body of a Sora rail?

66.   Who were the Suffetes in Carthaginian politics?

67.   What was the reply Thackeray made to a political opponent in an election who had said to Thackeray: "May the best man win"?

68.   What is the vernacular name of Tipperary?

69.   Ce Tacpatl Mixcoatl's son was a most important figure in Toltec history. What was his name?

70.   How many times had the Atlantic been crossed by air before Lindbergh made his solo flight?

71.   Find an illustration of Ulysses shooting an arrow into the heart of one of his wife's suitors.

72.   Where is there an account of the U.S. Dept. of the Interior which includes both an organization chart and a list of all the secretaries of the department?

73.   Identify Agnes Julie Fredrika von Krusenstjerna-Sprengel.

74.   Find a summary of the novel *The Wandering Jew*. Who wrote it?

75.   Quote several of George Washington's *Rules of Civility*.

76. Find simple diagrammatic illustrations of a water meter showing how it works and how to read it.

77. The Irish and American spelling of "whiskey" is different from the British and Canadian. What is the Gaelic form of the word and what is its meaning?

78. Who was the commander of the 400 American settlers who were massacred in the Wyoming Valley Battle of 1778?

79. Find a picture of the "Big Three," Stalin, Churchill, and Roosevelt, meeting at Yalta in 1945.

80. Where could one find both a short definition and a long, detailed article on aeronautical engineering?

81. Where can I find full-color overlays showing the anatomy of a grass frog?

82. Where would you find rules for the card game, skat?

83. Where would you look to find a picture of the spires of the cathedral in Chartres, France?

84. Where would you look to find step-by-step instructions for building a dam?

85. Where would you look to find the type of cartoons drawn by the Frenchman, Daumier?

86. Where could you find a colored picture of the state flag, flower and bird of Delaware?

87. Find an article on Albert Einstein with a portrait and a signature facsimile.

88. Where could you find a picture of the Puli working dog?

89. Where could you find the rules for the sport of rugby?

90.   Where would you find pictures of the buildings of interest in Frascati, Italy?

91.   Where could you find the real name and a short biography of Cardinale Gaetano?

92.   Locate a picture of a dartboard.

93.   Find an illustrated article on the life and culture of ancient Greece with a fact index for young readers.

94.   Hathor was a goddess in which mythology?

95.   Where could you find a section on history covering both America and the rest of the world with examination questions at the end?

96.   What is the name of the curved basket used in the sport of jai alai?

97.   Who was Josephus Nelson Larned?

98.   Where can I find an article on the April Theses of V.I. Lenin?

99.   Middletown, New York was incorporated in what year?

100. Locate a brief discussion of the merits of the paperback novel.

101. Find an article on Wolfgang Amadeus Mozart with a portrait.

102. What is the pronunciation of Persepolis?

103. Find an identification of "Back Bay" in Boston.

104. For which poem is the English poet, William Shenstone, best known?

105. Where may I find a fairly lengthy entry on Rabelais with a bibliography of works about him?

106.   Find a simply written, signed article entitled "How to Do Research," with a list of selected reference books.

107.   Find a signed article on trademarks with familiar illustrations and information on U.S. federal and state trademark laws.

108.   Locate an illustrated article for children on the United Nations.

109.   Where could you find an outline for the study of the history of the U.S.?

110.   Locate an article on the Vatican with a map and excellent plates.

111.   Locate an article about George Washington with numerous illustrations, a copy of his farewell address, and a bibliography of books and films about him.

112.   What was named for Bertha Krupp?

113.   Find an illustrated article on nursery rhymes with a fact index for young readers.

114.   I would like a description, with a map, of the city of Mainz.

115.   I want a brief and general explanation of the Haber process.

116.   Find the birth date of Julius Caesar.

117.   What are the main patterns and colors used in Bulgarian embroidery?

118.   What was the title of Virginia Woolf's first novel?

119.   What were the inclusive dates of the rule of the House of Stuart over England?

120.   Where would you look for a self-educating course on botany?

121.   Who was the presidential candidate of the Democratic Party in 1916?

122.	What are the three main types of English architecture?

123.	How many books are in the New York Public Library?

124.	How was the population of the world distributed in the 1500s?

125.	What are the names of the important libraries in Florence, Italy?

126.	An instructor is seeking a discussion and perhaps a summary of Diderot's *Le Neveu de Rameau,* a satire in dialogue. Can you help him?

127.	A geography student needs to know the location of an island called Crabes in the nineteenth century.

128.	Which book of the Old Testament relates the tale of "The Grateful Dead"?

129.	Where can I find quotations from Voltaire, Rabelais, and Racine?

130.	A political science student needs information about the Finnish Workers' party. Can you help him?

131.	What caused Pecos Bill's death?

132.	How is the city of Seville arranged?

133.	What are the names and characteristics of several of the newer forms of painting?

134.	What type of dress was worn in the French court around 1430?

135.	Where can I find some historical background on Dieppe prior to the Allied Commando Raid in World War II?

136.	A graduate student is doing research on the official colonial policy immediately prior to the fall of Dienbienphu. Where could he look for information?

137.	What painters have done paintings of Stephen the martyr?

138.   What is Napoleon holding in Canova's statue?

139.   A student asks you for a study aid which is in outline form because his friend found one in an encyclopedia, but neither remembers the name of the encyclopedia. Can you help him?

140.   What was the principal event of the year 79 A.D.?

141.   With which Roman god is the Greek god Zeus identified?

142.   Can you find a table of vertebrates?

143.   A high school student needs a fuller discussion of asteroids than a dictionary contains. What source would provide a simple, nontechnical discussion?

144.   What is the basis of the Islamic calendar?

145.   Find illustrated articles for children on the Indian Wars with a list of related articles and a study outline.

146.   Who was called "Old Rough and Ready"?

147.   Who wrote *The Damnation of Theron Ware* ?

148.   What is the length of the Nile River?

149.   Locate articles on Fourier analysis.

150.   Find an article on American life insurance written by an expert.

151.   Find a list of how-to-do-it books for the amateur photographer.

152.   Find an article on Albia, Iowa.

153.   Locate a long and detailed article on art in the Western world.

154.   Where are the Beaver Islands?

155.   How is the surname "Campinchi" pronounced?

156. Find a brief biography of Alfredo Casella, an Italian composer who died in 1947.

157. Find an extensive selection of examination questions on the subject of literature.

158. Find a bibliography on agriculture to be used for self-study.

159. Find a diagram of a tachometer.

160. Locate a map of Alaska, suitable for children.

161. How is the name of the Aisne River pronounced?

162. How is the word, "calico," pronounced?

163. Find a picture of an adobe hut.

164. Find articles with poems and stories interspersed to capture children's attention.

165. Find an article attempting to help children feel how Eskimos live.

166. Find an illustrated article with several maps and a graded bibliography on North Dakota, suitable for children.

167. Who was Ceres?

168. Find a fact summary in the index of an encyclopedia for the U.S. with several illustrations suitable for children.

169. Find a brief explanation of Confucianism complete with pronunciation.

170. Locate an in-depth article on Soviet drama.

171. Find an article about the moon designed to capture and hold a child's attention.

172. Find a table of mythological associations.

173.   Locate an article on farming aimed at a seventh grade student.

174.   Find selected, annotated bibliographies on history, law, political science and government conveniently located in a single volume.

175.   Which encyclopedia index provides definitions and basic facts?

176.   Who was Gluskabe?

177.   Find a study aid in outline form for children.

178.   Which encyclopedia has all the articles on biology together?

179.   Find an article for a fifth grade student interested in Italy.

180.   Find an article written from the Communist viewpoint on the Vietnam War.

181.   Which encyclopedia has games, puzzles and riddles for young children?

182.   Find an outline of knowledge.

183.   Find a colored reproduction of the initial page of "Purgatoria" from Dante's *Divine Comedy*.

184.   Find a classified bibliography on biology which would be at the junior college level and which would show many facets of the subject, such as "botany" and "microbiology" at the end of the set.

185.   Find the date of birth of George Washington in the index of an encyclopedia.

186.   Find a long discussion on sculpture of all times and places with many plates and an extensive bibliography.

187.   Locate a short biography of Melingue, a nineteenth-century French actor and sculptor.

188. Find a biography of Emerson Hough.

189. Find an article on the FCC.

190. Locate an article on the life of Marconi.

191. Who invented the first successful fountain pen?

192. Find a list of weights per bushel for various grains and fruits.

193. Is all of Lower California part of Mexico?

194. Who was Antoine Lavoisier?

195. Find an article on the International Red Cross.

196. Find pictures of various subhuman primates.

197. Find biographies of Roger Bacon and Francis Bacon.

198. How much does one gallon of water weigh?

199. Find a summary of events which occurred in the sixteenth century.

200. Find some general information on Lockport, New York.

201. Find the name of an important person in New York City for a student who needs to make a report on such a person.

202. Who were Laplace and Mayer?

203. What were the names of Henry VIII's wives?

204. Who was Queen Victoria's mother?

205. Find a biography of Patrick Henry for a child.

206. Find an article on fate and free will.

207. Find a description of life on Southern plantations for a child.

208.   Find a biography of Max Planck.

209.   What is the largest bell in the world?

210.   What is the meaning of "Israfel"?

211.   Find an article on the Imperial Valley.

212.   Find an article on H. Sienkiewicz.

213.   Find a picture of Martin Luther.

214.   Where is St. Paul's Cathedral?

215.   Find a short method of figuring interest.

216.   Is Michigan an Indian word and what is the meaning?

217.   Who was the Man in the Iron Mask?

218.   Who were Héloise and Abélard?

219.   Identify Nizam al Mulk.

220.   What is the longest river in the world?

221.   Were the Swedes Mongols?

222.   How does one figure extra cube roots by logarithms?

223.   How long does it take a baby elephant to mature?

224.   Which is harder, glass or steel?

225.   Who was Alexander VI?

226.   What is the national flower of Scotland?

227.   What are the true colors of the peacock?

228.   Find a picture of a Dutch windmill.

229.   Compare rainfall in England and France.

230.   Find some information on cavemen appropriate for children.

231.   What part of the U.S. produces the most cranberries?

232.   Find an article on cocoa.

233.   Find a history of the X-ray.

234.   In what year was Albert Einstein born?

235.   How is steel processed?

236.   Find a short history of Sweden.

237.   Locate a history of national parks.

238.   Find a picture of a fawn.

239.   Find a biography of Willa Cather.

240.   Do penguins have feathers on their flippers?

241.   Find instructions on how to form Roman numerals through 500.

242.   Find a biography of James Bright.

243.   Who was the first U.S. president not born a British subject?

244.   What were the names of Admiral Peary's ships?

245.   Find a general article on silkworms.

246.   Find a history of ballet in Australia.

247.   For what is Trinidad noted?

248.   Locate pictures of flags from Latin American countries.

249.   What is the abbreviation for London?

250.   What is the name of the red cape used in bull fighting?

251.   What are the major sports in England?

252.   What was the date when Hitler invaded Poland?

253.   What are the most important provisions of the Magna Carta, the Bill of Rights, and the Petition of Rights?

254.   Find some information on the role of Canada in World War I.

255.   What is the word for a polygon of nine sides?

256.   Find a picture of the chambered nautilus showing the chambers.

257.   Find a biography of Woodrow Wilson for a small boy.

258.   Find a biography of John Rutledge.

259.   What did Florence Nightingale wear during the Crimean War?

260.   Find pictures of gypsies' costumes.

261.   Who painted "Napoleon Visiting the Pest House at Jaffa"?

262.   Why do people throw rice at weddings?

263.   Find a list of the state birds and flowers.

264.   Find information on the Leni-Lenape tribe of Indians.

265.   Locate information on the port of Huelva in Spain.

266.   Find a map showing the resources of New Jersey.

267.   When did Henry Ford die?

268.   When did Franklin Roosevelt die?

269.   Find a history of the game of bridge.

270. Where was Ernie Pyle killed?

271. What are the requirements for membership in the American Legion?

272. What were the major causes of World War I?

273. What are the procedures for a trial by jury?

274. When was the first rural mail delivery?

275. Find data on videodisks.

276. Which encyclopedia has a "Colorpedia"?

277. Locate an article on "iconoclasm" appropriate for a junior high school student.

278. My friend and I are having a disagreement over the pronunciation of the composer Gabriel Fauré's name. Can you tell us the actual pronunciation?

279. What is the origin of falconing?

280. Who is Hester Prynne?

281. Where could I find an explanation of "math anxiety" in women and girls?

282. Where was Confucius born?

283. What equipment was used by the U.S. to break secret codes during World War II?

284. When was Oliver Cromwell appointed by parliament commander-in-chief of all the forces of the Commonwealth?

285. What are the most important cardiac glycosides in medicine?

286. I need an explanation of irrigation appropriate for an 8th grader.

287.   What is a "displaced homemaker"?

288.   Who were some of the first female orchestral conductors?

289.   Where can I find information on the participation of women in the political process?

290.   One of my more literate friends referred to "Luke Frugal" in one of our discussions. Who is this Frugal guy? I didn't want my friend to know I didn't know who he was talking about.

291.   Did the University of Michigan have a School of Homeopathic Medicine in 1849?

292.   Locate a concise chronological dateline of all the periods of English literature and all the writers who fit into those periods.

293.   I am looking for information on Soviet propaganda regarding the freedom of access to public libraries after the October 1917 Revolution.

294.   What are the birth and death dates of English novelist Jane Austen?

295.   What is the difference between a cyclone and an anticyclone?

296.   I need some really good information on types of ecosystems, but I don't have time to read a book.

297.   Where could I find a short discussion of the "Queen Bee Syndrome," a feminist issue?

298.   What was René Clair's original name?

299.   I know that Charles Babbage made a machine called the Difference Engine, but what other machines did he make?

300.   Where can I find information on the history of Colne, a small town in Lancashire, England?

301. Where can one find brief information about British Political
      parties?

302. Who were some noted female novelists of the 1920s?

303. When William Penn was laying out the city of Philadelphia, he
      planned for 5 squares, one in the center of the city and 4 in each
      quadrant. What are they?

304. Where can I find an article on the Protestant Reformation
      written by a foremost scholar?

305. I need a general article on NASA.

306. I know an okapi is in the giraffe family, but does it look like a
      giraffe? Show me a color picture of one.

307. Who was born in Shrewsbury, MA?

308. I need to find some information on anti-feminist movements.
      I'm starting a research project and need to get some basic
      names, dates and organizations for further research.

309. When was the Kanto Earthquake in Japan?

310. Do algae produce oxygen?

311. When was Claude Monet born and when did he die?

312. I'm looking for any painting that depicts the Deposition from
      the Cross.

313. Where would you find information on the treatment of rape in
      literature and law in the Medieval era?

314. What are the philanthropic bequests of Andrew Carnegie? I
      need a little bit (about a paragraph) of information on each.

Reference Materials

Academic American Encyclopedia
Britannica Junior Encyclopaedia
Brockhaus Enzyklopaedie
Chambers's Encyclopaedia
Childcraft
Collier's Encyclopedia
Compton's Encyclopedia
Compton's Precyclopedia
Enciclopedia italiana di scienze, lettere ed arti
Enciclopedia universal ilustrada Europeo-Americana (Espasa)
Encyclopaedia Britannica
Encyclopedia Americana
Encyclopedia of Asian History
Everyman's Encyclopedia
Grand Larousse encyclopédique
La grande encyclopédie
Great Soviet Encyclopedia
Lincoln Library of Essential Information
Merit Students Encyclopedia
New Century Cyclopedia of Names
New Columbia Encyclopedia
New Encyclopedia Britannica
Random House Encyclopedia
Women's Studies Encyclopedia
World Book Encyclopedia

CHAPTER 2

YEARBOOKS

Reference Interviews

Patron #1.   A man.

Patron: I need your help with three questions. First, I'd like to
             know the number of square miles in the U.S. and
             Canada.
Librarian: Do you want the U.S. with Hawaii and Alaska or just
             the 48 states?
Patron: Could I have both?
Librarian: It's also divided by land and water. Do you want it
             together or divided?
Patron: Divided. Now, do you have the area of the Great
             Lakes?
Librarian: Do you want the area of the drainage basin or just the
             water?
Patron: Just the water.
Librarian: Are you using these figures for a paper or something?
Patron: Yes, I'm comparing the population of certain states as a
             percentage of the total land area and population. Now I
             need the population of the U.S. and Canada—the most
             recent figures possible.

             Which sources would you check to answer these
             questions?

Patron #2.   A college student.

Patron: I want to find some information on McCormick Place.
Librarian: Is that a building?
Patron: Yes.
Librarian: Do you know where it's located?

Patron:	Chicago.
Librarian:	Just what did you want to know about the building?
Patron:	I'd like to know when it burned down.
Librarian:	Do you have any general idea of how recently this happened?
Patron:	In this century.

Where would you look?

Patron #3.   A man.

Patron:	Did Michigan go to Pasadena in 1967?
Librarian:	You mean did The University of Michigan go to the Rose Bowl in 1967?
Patron:	Yes.

Where would you look?

Patron #4.   A junior high school boy.

Patron:	Do you have any lists of prizes?
Librarian:	What sort of prizes do you mean? Suggestions for party prizes or what?
Patron:	Well, you see, I've got this list of guys—scientists and authors—and they won prizes, Nobel and Pulitzer, and I've got to find out when they won them.

Where could the dates be found?

Patron #5.   A student.

Patron:	I would like to know where I can find the results of the 1968 national election for president of the U.S.
Librarian:	Is this for your government class?
Patron:	Yes, and I would like to know about the unsuccessful candidates, too, and the names of the other parties.
Librarian:	Oh, you mean like the Socialist Party?
Patron:	Yes.

Where could this information be found?

Patron #6.   A high school student.

Patron: Where can I find a short article on Somaliland?
Librarian: You don't want to use the encyclopedias?
Patron: No, those articles are too long.

               Where would you look for brief information?

Patron #7.   A man.

Patron: Where could I find the population of some cities?
Librarian: Which cities?
Patron: Some of the large cities in the U.S., like Detroit and
               Cleveland.

               Where would you look?

Reference Questions

1. Find the address of the American Medical Association.

2. What is the Jewish population of Argentina?

3. Name the U.N. representatives from Japan.

4. Who is the chair of the British Broadcasting Corporation?

5. Did Babe Ruth ever hit 60 home runs in one year?

6. Who is the leader of the Communist party in Australia?

7. Where is there the most complete list of newspapers and
    magazines published in British Columbia?

8. Who is the keeper of Oriental Printed Books and Manuscripts in
    the British Library?

9. Find a list of Cuba's national holidays.

10. What are the names and addresses of the newspapers and periodicals published in Ceylon?

11. What are the annual fees at Eton College in Windsor, England?

12. Locate a brief summary of the history of dictatorships in Central America.

13. What are the major sources of revenue of Gibraltar?

14. What is the vernacular name of the Hashemite kingdom of Jordan?

15. What is the highest building in the world?

16. What are some of the major banks of Iceland?

17. What are the gasoline taxes in Illinois?

18. What is the maximum number of representatives in India's House of People?

19. In terms of membership, which are the biggest churches in Ireland, and what are the names of their chief officers?

20. How many telephones are there in Japan?

21. When did the English pirate Sharpe sack La Serena, Chile?

22. Which public libraries are members of the Yukon Regional Library System?

23. What is the address of the Librarie Ernest Flammarion in Paris?

24. Find a brief history and description of the Victoria Cross medal of honor.

25. What is the lowest temperature on record in Minneapolis?

26. What is the height of Mt. Everest?

27. Who is the director of the National Gallery in London?

28. What are the inheritance taxes in the State of New Jersey?

29. How many presidents of the U.S. have received Nobel prizes?

30. How many motor vehicles are registered in Nova Scotia?

31. Who were the poets laureate of England in the 17th century?

32. What is the full title of the pope?

33. What are the chief Portuguese insurance companies?

34. Locate a perpetual calendar which covers the dates January 1st, 1 A.D. to December 31st, 2000 A.D. On which day of the week did April 17, 1990 fall?

35. When does the month of Ramadan begin this year?

36. What is the Roman numeral for 1,000,000?

37. What is the Indian rupee worth in American money? What other coins are used in India?

38. What is the population of the capital of Saudi Arabia?

39. What is Sikkim and how large is it?

40. What is the national anthem of Spain?

41. In what cities are the Sugar Bowl and the Orange Bowl played?

42. Who holds the title of Duke of St. Alban's?

43. Find the text of the Charter of the United Nations.

44. What is the address of the Universal Postal Union?

45.   Find a list of the administrative officials and faculty of the University of New Brunswick.

46.   Who was the first occupant of the White House?

47.   How is a woman's rank determined in the order of precedence in England?

48.   What is the name of the present Archbishop of Canterbury?

49.   What is the address of the Canadian embassy in Burma?

50.   Locate a series of star maps which chart the movement of the constellations from January to December.

51.   What important events took place in horse racing in Britain two years ago?

52.   Where could you find the name of the president and present address of the Eaton Insurance Company of Toronto, Canada?

53.   What are the names of the political parties in Luxembourg?

54.   Find a chart showing Postmaster Generals by administration, George Washington to the present.

55.   Where could one find recent statistics on transportation in Canada?

56.   What important matters were discussed at the United Nations last year?

57.   Does the U.S.S.R. have an embassy in Upper Volta?

58.   What are the annuities paid various members of the Royal Family of England?

59.   I would like a daily chronology of the major world events for a given year in the past decade.

60. How many people in Ontario are employed in the fishing industry?

61. Who are the delegates to the Economic and Social Council of the United Nations?

62. What are the names of the representatives of Tunisia to Great Britain?

63. What is the orbital velocity and the synodical period of Mercury?

64. What is the type of government of Morocco?

65. How many telephones (per 100 population) are there in Canada?

66. Who is the president of Zambia?

67. Who won the Nobel prize in physics last year?

68. Where can I find a description of Caracas?

69. Who is the President of the Canadian Pacific Railway?

70. Do you have a copy of the text of the Tashkent Declaration signed by Shastri before he died?

71. What is the population of the city of Birmingham, England, and who is its Lord Mayor?

72. Where is there a list of the countries in which Spain maintains diplomatic representatives?

73. Who is the honorary president of the Presidium of the World Council of Churches?

74. At what time will the sun rise in Ottawa on November 6?

75. What major changes took place last year in the Swiss economy?

76.   Who was awarded the Nobel prizes in Chemistry last year?

77.   Find the address of the International Bar Association.

78.   What is the name of the leading newspaper in Oslo, Norway?

79.   Where can I find statistics on the production of fur in Canada?

80.   What is the high and low tide for the coastal city of Aberdeen, Scotland?

81.   Who is the Ambassador of Belgium to Canada?

82.   What is the Gross National Product of Gabon?

83.   I am going to be making a trip to Lima, Peru in October. I plan to be there for two months. What sort of clothes should I take?

84.   Can you tell me where I might find a description of the various government agencies which are conducting surveying and mapping in Canada?

85.   Where can one find information on the World Council of Churches?

86.   Where can one find information on the North Atlantic Treaty Organization?

87.   What are the principal industries of Iraq?

88.   What is the amount of pay of a vice-admiral in the Navy with twelve years of service?

89.   Find an article on last year's domestic events in Iran with a brief summary of data on that country.

90.   Locate a world survey of last year's literature presented by country.

91.   What percentage of Danes were born in Denmark?

92. Locate an overview of the judicial system in the Netherlands.

93. Is *The Times* of India a Nationalist newspaper?

94. Where would you find a short history of Tobago?

95. Find a list of museums in Kingston, Jamaica.

96. Is the tap water safe to drink in the Netherlands Antilles?

97. Does Portugal use the metric system?

98. What are the world's top fifty banks?

99. Where may I find brief information about banking in Canada?

100. What was the major literary event of the Western world between 900-800 B.C.?

101. Who are Algeria's cabinet members?

102. Locate information on education in Nauru.

103. What were the results of the last general election in Belgium?

104. Locate a street map of Rio de Janeiro.

105. Locate a news summary of the last New York Democratic primary.

106. Locate the scores of the World Series games from 1903 to the present.

107. What is the currency of Norway?

108. What are the programs of Malta's two leading political parties?

109. Who won the first Indianapolis 500 race?

110. What is the predominant religion in Afghanistan?

111.   When is the rainy season in Trinidad?

112.   Which country produced the most steel last year?

113.   How many ships are in Sri Lanka's navy?

114.   Who are the assistant bishops at Canterbury?

115.   Find a map of La Paz, Bolivia, with a discussion of points of interest.

116.   Which players have won the Grand Slam of Tennis? What requirements must be met to earn this honor?

117.   Find a list of educational institutions and their staffs in Canada.

118.   What is the total value of food imported into Finland?

119.   Who is the U.S. ambassador to the Soviet Union?

120.   What are some of the new plays which have opened in New York recently?

121.   Who are the senators and representatives from New York?

122.   How many Confucianists live in Fiji?

123.   Find a picture of the flag of the president of the U.S.

124.   Find a list of weights and measures in Great Britain.

125.   What is the evening star now?

126.   How long was Alfred the Great king of England?

127.   Locate some information about fraternities.

128.   Who is the chairperson of the American Red Cross?

129.   When did the U.S. adopt woman's suffrage?

130. What is the religion of Pakistan?

131. What is the capital of Oregon?

132. Find a list of state governors.

133. What is the postage to foreign countries?

134. Find a list of the cabinet officers.

135. Where is the largest telescope in the world?

136. What are the rules for the proper display of the American flag?

137. Who was the third vice-president of the U.S. and what was his political affiliation?

138. Can the son of a president be elected president?

139. How has the cost of living risen for the past ten years?

140. What is the average yearly salary for teachers in the U.S.?

141. What is the deepest oil well in the world?

142. What gifts are appropriate for a thirtieth wedding anniversary?

143. On what day in 1791 did The Bill of Rights go into effect?

144. When will Easter be next year?

145. When was Easter in 1924?

146. What are the largest public libraries in the U.S.?

147. What was the date of the first Tuesday after the first Monday in 1942?

148. Who is the Speaker of the House of Representatives?

149. What are the names of the New Jersey representatives in the U.S. Congress?

150. Is John "Blood" McNally in the Pro Football Hall of Fame?

151. Find a summary of the 1790 census of New York state.

152. What is the population of Cleveland?

153. What is the date, MDCCCXCIV?

154. What are the names of the associate justices of the U.S. Supreme Court?

155. When has the U.S. declared war against various countries?

156. Find a list of national holidays of the U.S.

157. What is the public debt of the U.S.?

158. Find summaries of divorce laws in various states.

159. Which of the Great Lakes is the largest?

160. Which athlete earned the most money last year?

161. Find a picture of the flag of India.

162. Locate the exact wording of the Pledge of Allegiance.

163. When was the National Speleological Society formed?

164. What are the ten largest cities in the U.S.?

165. What is the postal rate on books?

166. What was the maiden name of Millard Fillmore's first wife?

167. What is the meaning of a dash over a Roman numeral?

168. When is Flag Day?

169.   What are the marriage laws in Indiana?

170.   What were the principal events 100 years ago?

171.   What is the fifteenth wedding anniversary called?

172.   What is the origin of the names of the states?

173.   How do the various states compare in national forests?

174.   What is the value of a peso?

175.   What are the names of the National Memorials?

176.   What are the gasoline taxes in the various states?

177.   How many time zones does Greenland have?

178.   What is the largest dam in the world?

179.   How old is the monarch of the Netherlands?

180.   Find a list of all the senators and representatives in the present Congress.

181.   Does Portugal produce more wine than olive oil?

182.   What are the names of the hotels in Morelia, Mexico?

183.   What years was Chester Arthur president?

184.   What are the immigration laws of the U.S.?

185.   Who have won the Pulitzer prizes for the past ten years?

186.   Find the text of the Declaration of Independence.

187.   What is the ratio of divorces to marriages?

188.   How many electoral votes does Illinois have?

189.   How many people are enrolled in Blue Cross?

190.   How often does Tuttle's Comet reappear to Earth observers?

191.   How much money was appropriated for defense by the last Congress?

192.   How many stripes does the Coast Guard insignia for an ensign carry?

193.   What is the boiling point of alcohol?

194.   Can Easter ever be on March 29?

195.   What New York plays have had the longest runs?

196.   What magazine has the largest circulation?

197.   Locate a list of geologic periods.

198.   What is the record high and low in temperature for Miami?

199.   What are the territories and dependencies of the U.S.?

200.   What is the name of the congressperson from this district?

201.   How long is the Alaskan Highway?

202.   How many accidental deaths were there last year in the U.S.?

203.   Find a list of famous planetariums.

204.   What is the name of the national anthem of Sweden?

205.   Find a list of famous fires.

206.   What was the increase of the black population in the U.S. from the first census to the Civil War?

207.   What was the date of the Cocoanut Grove fire?

208.   Find information on an event which happened in the U.S. a month ago.

209.   Who is the current director of public records for Great Britain?

210.   What is the platform of the Australian Labor Party?

211.   What are the names of the foreign banks which have branch offices in Japan?

212.   On what date will Easter be observed next year?

213.   What were some of the major events in the coal industry last year?

214.   What were some of the major events in Britain last month?

215.   I would like an overview of what happened to Finland politically during World War II.

216.   What is the current population of Ottawa, the Canadian capital?

217.   I'd like an overview of what happened in New Zealand in 1970.

218.   What newspapers are published in English in Singapore, and what are their addresses?

219.   What is the population of Taiwan (Republic of China)?

220.   From what product does São Tomé and Principe receive the majority of its exported earnings?

221.   How large is the Pentagon building, in square feet?

222.   I need to know what countries are members of the United Nations Economic Commission for Europe.

223.   Where may one find general information about the International Telecommunications Union?

224.   How many people died in Michigan in 1989?

225.   Where can I find the name and address for the Chamber of
       Commerce in Oslo, Norway?

226.   Where can I find a list of participants and scores for the Rose
       Bowl since its inception in 1902? What I really need to know is
       what school has won the most Rose Bowls?

227.   Is a prepositional phrase one of the eight parts of speech?

228.   How many suspension bridges exist in North America, and
       where are they located?

229.   Where was the first circulating library in the U.S. and when did
       it start?

230.   Where can I find a list of collective names for animals such as a
       gaggle of geese?

231.   What is the address of the Saskatchewan Court of Appeals?

232.   I recently went to Toronto for vacation. Can I get a room tax
       rebate?

233.   I'd like to make a brief record of what was going on in the U.S.
       and world the week my daughter was born, on March 31, 1991.
       Where could I find this?

234.   Where can you have your camera fixed in Buenos Aires?

235.   How do I clean the tartar off my cat's teeth?

236.   Where can I find information on the Canadian government's
       role in the funding of science and technology research and
       development since 1990?

237.   In which book can one find a brief biography of Boris Yeltsin?

238.   What form of government does Australia have?

239.   What is the governing party of Canada?

240. Where would I look to find what safety procedure to follow during a hurricane?

241. I need a list of art galleries in Canada.

242. I want to join the Yukon Badminton Association. Can you find the address so I can write them and get information on membership requirements?

243. What is the telephone number for the facsimile machine at the Canadian Embassy in the Peoples' Republic of China?

244. What is the government in Singapore and who is the leader?

245. How many moviegoers were there in Hong Kong in 1989?

246. On what day did the Gulf War begin?

247. What were the best-selling books of 1990?

248. What was the ruling party in South Korea for 1991?

249. Where can you find current practical travel information as well as cultural and historical information on the area of Patagonia in Argentina?

250. What is the current annual salary of members of the Canadian senate?

Reference Materials

Americana Annual
Annual Register
Annual Register of World Events
Britannica Book of the Year
Canada Year Book
Canadian Almanac and Directory

CIA World Factbook
Collier's Encyclopedia Yearbook
Collier's Yearbook
Compton Yearbook
Europa World Year Book
Europa Year Book
Facts on File
Information Please Almanac
International Yearbook and Statesmen's Who's Who
Keesing's Contemporary Archives
N.Y. Public Library Desk Reference
Political Handbook and Atlas of the World
South American Handbook
State Dept. Travel Advisories
Statesman's Year-Book
Whitaker's Almanac
World Affairs Report
World Almanac
World Book Year Book
Yearkbook of the United Nations

CHAPTER 3

STATISTICAL SOURCES

Reference Interviews

Patron #1.   A woman.

Patron:	I need information on budgets.
Librarian:	How to make a budget or statistics on budgets?
Patron:	What I want is something on budgets for families; statistics, I guess.
Librarian:	Then you want budget figures for families in the U.S.?
Patron:	Well, I don't really know. You see, I'm having an argument, discussion really, with my husband on how much money we should spend on different things, and I thought if I could find out what other families like us spend to live comfortably it would help me to win.

Where would you look for this information?

Patron #2.   A young high school girl.

Patron:	I need to find some election results.
Librarian:	Do you need to have state or federal election results?
Patron:	I need them for the election of Madison.
Librarian:	Let's see. That was 18--?
Patron:	It was in 1812.
Librarian:	You want the election results for the presidential election of 1812. Do you just want the total electoral vote or state by state?
Patron:	I need the state by state vote.

Where could this information be found?

Patron #3.   A student.

Patron: Where can I find statistics on immigration?
Librarian: Do you want statistical quotas from countries or do you
                 want actual immigrants admitted from all countries or
                 both?
Patron: I want information on actual immigrants admitted from
                 all countries.

                 Where would you look?

Reference Questions

1.   What was the estimated population of the American colonies in
     1630?

2.   What was the average population per household in Ann Arbor
     in 1970?

3.   What was the death rate among the male population of
     Massachusetts in 1895?

4.   What was the number of German immigrants from 1850-1870?

5.   How many Lithuanian immigrants were living in the U.S. in
     1850?

6.   How many marriages took place in Alaska and New York in
     1960 and 1970?

7.   How much money was spent by the Navy Department in 1792?

8.   Does Portland, Maine have more clear days during the year than
     Detroit?

9.   What was the tonnage of sailing vessels of the U.S. Merchant
     Marine in 1866?

10. How much did the federal government spend on national defense in 1942?

11. Find general statistics about the characteristics of new, privately-owned one-family homes in the U.S. which are fairly recent.

12. What is the average August temperature of Philadelphia?

13. What was the population of the Standard Metropolitan Areas in the last census of the U.S.?

14. Find the figures for unemployment in the first half of the twentieth century in the U.S.

15. Find the average income for an industrial worker in 1930 in the U.S.

16. What is the voting population of California?

17. What is the divorce rate in Japan?

18. Find the number of Chinese immigrants to the U.S. in 1850.

19. How many institutions of higher education were there in the U.S. in 1946?

20. What was the population of New York City in 1900?

21. How many acres of sugar beets are harvested annually in the U.S.?

22. Where could I find a list of money conversion co-efficients and factors?

23. What was the amount of the total defense contract awards made last year in the U.S.?

24. What is the amount of coffee production in Uganda?

25. What was the number of pounds of raw silk exported from North and South Carolina in 1750?

26. What was the total income of U.S. life insurance companies in 1898?

27. What is the population of Prokopyesk, Russia?

28. What was the average farm wage, per month, in the U.S. in 1920 for a hand living with a farmer?

29. Which is more populous: Argentina, Colombia, or Burma?

30. What was the population of the U.S. in 1962?

31. How many telephones are in use in Belgium?

32. What was the average annual salary of college teachers in the U.S. in 1940?

33. What is the birth rate in Sweden?

34. What was the average number of rooms of a new, one-family home in the U.S. in 1950?

35. How many tons of tin were produced in Bolivia two years ago?

36. What is the average life expectancy for men in India?

37. How many doctoral degrees in psychology were conferred by U.S. institutions in 1981? What percent of the recipients were female?

38. How many renter-occupied housing units with more than one bathroom are there in Albany, New York?

39. How many non-whites own their own farms in Rhode Island?

40. What were the average annual earnings per full-time employee in the U.S. by major industry for 1938?

41. What was the acreage of oats harvested for 1926-30 in the U.S.?

42. How many banks were there in the U.S. in 1933?

43. How many gasoline service stations are there in Rapid City, South Dakota?

44. What was the retail value of microwave ovens produced in the U.S. in 1978?

45. How many Methodists were there in the U.S. in 1936?

46. Find the population of Santa Monica, California for each decade since 1890.

47. What is the average age at marriage for a male in New Zealand?

48. How much beer was produced in New Zealand each year for the past ten years?

49. What was China's crude death rate in 1935?

50. What was the price of lead in the United Kingdom month before last?

51. How many Indians are there in Michigan?

52. What are the age and population characteristics of this county?

53. How many black people live in Pike County, Ohio?

54. How many people who are over eighteen live in this county?

55. How many Turks live in European Turkey?

56. Find the most recent figures available on unemployment in Denmark, Finland, and Sweden.

57. How many Germans immigrated to this country between 1850 and 1870?

58.   What is the total median income of families living in the South
      Atlantic states?

59.   What is the average number of rooms per housing unit in the
      city of Laredo, Texas?

60.   What is the college enrollment in New Jersey by county?

61.   How many acres of forest land were burned in the U.S. in forest
      fires in 1933?

62.   What were some of the major publications of the U.S.
      government on statistics on employment last year?

63.   How can I find statistics published in *Forbes* magazine last
      year?

64.   What is the average number of years of education completed by
      people in this congressional district?

65.   How has the population grown in the state of Arizona in the last
      thirty years and are all the new people old?

66.   How many people live in Dade County, Florida?

67.   Where would I find an index of statistics dealing with flowers
      and nursery products?

68.   What is the normal daily mean temperature of Little Rock,
      Arkansas?

69.   What is the total number of births in Sanborn County in South
      Dakota in 1984?

70.   Over the past three years, have factory production workers in
      Maryland earned more per hour than those in Michigan?

71.   What is the life expectancy at birth in El Salvador for a male?
      for a female?

72. What was the estimated total war cost of the Vietnam conflict for the U.S.?

73. What percentage of people in Kootenai County, Idaho were over 75 in 1984?

74. Has the total output and gross production of meat animals increased in the U.S. since 1972? If so, how much?

75. Of year-round housing units in Grand Traverse County, Michigan, what percentage had air conditioning as of April 1, 1980?

76. Where can I find information on rates of abortion for comparison of industrialized and non-industrialized countries?

77. Where can I find a breakdown of national forest acreage by state?

78. How many figs were produced in California in 1989?

79. What are the top five states which have the highest number of hazardous waste sites according to the Superfund Program?

80. What was the weekly diet of slaves in the U.S. before the Civil War?

81. Where can I find the projected enrollment of students in U.S. public schools for the year 2000?

82. What was the percentage increase in American households possessing television sets between 1950 and 1960?

83. I'm doing a paper on the recession, and I want to find out if more people are moonlighting at a second job.

84. Do most other countries have as many televisions as the U.S.?

85. What was the gross tonnage of U.S. merchant vessels in 1870?

86. How can I find out the relative numbers of children who will be entering the Detroit Public school system over the next five years?

87. Where would a population studies teacher find world population statistics for 1990?

88. What percentage of its petroleum does the U.S. import and from what countries?

89. Which country produced the most coffee in 1987, Columbia or Brazil?

90. Where would I look to find out how many women are holding state and local public offices?

91. I am interested in poultry production by state in the U.S. in 1989.

92. What was the difference in the number of military personnel on active duty each year during the Civil War between 1860 and 1866? I just need numbers, I am doing research for a book.

93. What is the population of the county seat of Slope County, ND?

94. How many U.S. veterans live in Utah, and how many of those are from World War II?

95. How many tourists visit Liechtenstein annually?

96. What is the normal daily minimum temperature of Juneau, Alaska, in January?

97. How many people immigrated from Germany and Russia, to the U.S. in 1905?

98. I want to find a worker's average earnings in manufacturing in the U.S. during the time frame of 1979 through 1987.

99. Where would you find abstracts for reports put out by the U.S. Bureau of Prisons under the Department of Justice?

100.   Where could I go to find some figures on occupational injuries
        among people who work in museums?

Reference Materials

American Statistics Index
CENDATA
Census of the U.S.
Commerce Department's Economic Bulletin Board and 1990 Census
        Data for Michigan?
Congressional District Data Book
County and City Data Book
Demographic Yearbook (U.N.)
Economic Almanac
Historical Statistics of the United States
Index to International Statistics
Statistical Abstract of the United States
Statistical Handbook on Women in America
Statistical Record of Black America
Statistical Reference Index
United Nations. Monthly Bulletin of Statistics
United Nations. Statistical Yearbook
USA Counties

CHAPTER 4

BIOGRAPHICAL SOURCES

Reference Interviews

Patron #1.   A high school boy.

Patron:	Where is your section on Stephen Crane?
Librarian:	Do you know what nationality he is?
Patron:	I don't know. He was a writer.
Librarian:	We can find out from Benet's *Reader's Encyclopedia*. It says he was an American, and lived from 1871-1900.
Patron:	That's what I thought. We're studying American literature.
Librarian:	Did you want books to check out on him, or reference books to look at here?
Patron:	Stuff to look at here, I guess. The report's due tomorrow.

What would you suggest?

Patron #2.   A woman.

Patron:	Where could I find some biographical information on S.S. Kresge? I already checked *Current Biography*. He isn't listed.
Librarian:	You could check for references to articles.

Where would you look?

Patron #3.   A high school boy.

Patron:	Where should I go to find out about authors?

Librarian:	Do you mean as a profession or did you have one specific author in mind?
Patron:	Just one—Forest McDonald.
Librarian:	Is he still alive?
Patron:	I don't know.
Librarian:	Well, when did he write a book that you know of?
Patron	The one I'm reading was copyrighted in 1958.
Librarian:	Is he an American then?
Patron:	Yes, I think so. At least it was published in the U.S.

Where would you go for information?

Patron #4.   A woman.

Patron:	Where do I find biographies of Americans?
Librarian:	We have several sources. Which person did you have in mind?
Patron:	Gordy Howe.
Librarian:	The hockey player?
Patron:	Yes.
Librarian:	Did you want a long or short article?
Patron:	Something longer, descriptive.

Where would you find lengthy articles?

Patron #5.   A college-aged boy.

Patron:	Do you have any books about motion pictures?
Librarian:	Yes, we have. I'll show them to you.
Patron:	Well, I don't see what I'm looking for in here. This is a difficult subject. I need some information about Akira Kurosawa.
Librarian:	I'm sorry to say that I don't recognize that name. Who is he?
Patron:	He's a movie director.
Librarian:	What nationality is he and is he living?
Patron:	Oh yes, he's alive. He's Japanese. I'm taking a course in the theater and I have to have some information about this guy. Not too much; enough for a two-page report.

Where would you check?

Patron #6.   A young high school girl.

Patron: My teacher has assigned each of us a contemporary
                 author to write on. Mine is Agatha Christie. Where
                 should I start looking?
Librarian: Did you check the card catalog?
Patron: Yes, they didn't have any works on her—just by her.
Librarian: *Contemporary Authors* would be the next logical place
                 to look.
Patron: There isn't anything on her.

Where would you go to next?

Patron #7.   A high school boy.

Patron: Where do you keep books on American authors?
Librarian: Did you have a specific author in mind?
Patron: Yes. Faulkner.
Librarian: Did you want a biography or a criticism?
Patron: Criticism. I'm writing this paper.
Librarian: Do you want to criticize a specific work then, or
                 Faulkner's work in general?
Patron: Just a couple of his novels.
Librarian: Did you check the card catalog under Faulkner?
Patron: Yes, but I don't know which books are good for what I
                 want. What I really want is a list of essays.

What would you suggest?

Patron #8.   A high school girl.

Patron: I need some information on Nelson Rockefeller.
Librarian: What kind of information do you want?
Patron: I just want something brief. I don't want to read a book
                 or anything.
Librarian: Do you want something general on his life or something
                 more specific on his political career and views?
Patron: I want something very brief just on his life.

Where would you look?

Patron #9. A high school girl.

Patron:	I need to find out the name of a legislator from 1789 to 1800.
Librarian:	Is this the U.S. Congress or some state legislature that you have in mind?
Patron:	The U.S. Congress. Both houses.
Librarian:	Do you want the name of just any one who was a legislator or a list of all of them?
Patron:	I want to see a list of all of them so that I can pick one to write a term paper on.

Where would you find a list?

Patron #10. A high school boy.

Patron:	I have to know about Karl Gauss.
Librarian:	What class is this for?
Patron:	Math.
Librarian:	Is he a mathematician?
Patron:	My teacher said he was a great mathematician who died sometime in the 1800's.
Librarian:	Was he an American?
Patron:	No. He was from Germany.

Where would you find a brief biography?

Patron #11. A woman.

Patron:	I just saw *Loves of Isadora* and I want to know when she was born.
Librarian:	Her full name was Isadora Duncan.
Patron:	That's right.

Where would you find the date?

Patron #12.   A student.

Patron: I want to know where I can find a critical essay on "The
                Duty of Civil Disobedience."
Librarian: Who wrote it?
Patron: It doesn't matter. I just need an essay.

                Where would you look?

Patron #13.   A high school boy.

Patron: This book has only a paragraph on Donald McKay.
                Where can I get more on him?
Librarian: Is he an American?
Patron: Yes.
Librarian: Dead?
Patron: Yes.

                Where would you look?

Patron #14.   A high school student.

Patron: I have to find out about Isaiah Thomas. Where can I
                look?
Librarian: How much information do you need?
Patron: I just need a little information about who he was, where
                he lived, when he was born. I don't want to read a
                whole book.
Librarian: Was he American?
Patron: Yes.
Librarian: Do you know when he lived?
Patron: I'm not sure, but I think in the colonial period.

                Where could you locate this information?

Patron #15.   A student.

Patron: Do you have anything on British authors?
Librarian: Did you want a general work or a specific author?
Patron: What I'm looking for is a biography of Shelley.

What would you suggest?

Patron #16.   A student.

Patron: I am writing a paper about J.D. Salinger and I don't
             know where to look for information.
Librarian: Were you interested in any specific work of the author
             or a general discussion of his life and work?
Patron: Just a general discussion, but I want to bring in his work
             and some criticism, too.

             Where would you go for biographies and critical
             articles?

Reference Questions

1.   Find the publishing history of Anne Bradstreet's poetry.

2.   Was Marie Emma Lajeunesse Albani's last name her maiden
     name, or married name?

3.   Name several famous students of the educator Benjamin Abbot.

4.   Who was the first rabbi to be ordained in the U.S.?

5.   What is the correct pronunciation of the name Alaud-din,
     second king of the Kilji dynasty of India?

6.   Who was Antonio Alaminos?

7.   Who was the mayor of Albany, N.Y. in 1796?

8.   When did the historian Bernard Andre live and what was his
     important work?

9.   Who was the first president of Antioch College?

10. Locate biographical material on Francis of Assisi that would be suitable for children.

11. What is the family name of Lord Beaverbrook?

12. What is the date of birth of Georges Bidault?

13. Who received the Brewster medal in 1921?

14. Who was governor of California in 1911?

15. What are the chief works of Louis Ferdinand Céline?

16. Where was Frances Bano Chance born?

17. Who was the founder of the first county jail library?

18. Name several noteworthy legal annotators born in the U.S.

19. Who are some of the most distinguished American conductors of the past?

20. Who was Speaker of the House in the 73rd Congress, 1933?

21. Who got the Congressional Gold Medal in 1777 for the surrender of Burgoyne?

22. Who was U.S. Ambassador to Costa Rica in 1853?

23. What was the title of Richard Crashaw's first volume of poetry?

24. Find a biography of Arthur R. Cushny, died 1926, formerly of The University of Michigan.

25. Who wrote a book about composers containing a discussion of Ingolf Dahl? It was titled *U.S. Composers* or *North American Composers,* the patron believes.

26. What library magazine carried an obituary of Test Dalton in 1946?

27. What was the War of the Dictionaries?

28. What is the importance of Paul A. Dirac?

29. Find a facsimile of Walt Disney's signature.

30. When was Douglas Fairbanks's picture, *The Black Pirate,* produced?

31. Who was the maternal grandfather of Samuel Fairclough, nonconformist divine?

32. What are the publications of Max Forster?

33. What scientific work was done by Ferdinand André Fouqué?

34. Did Eleanor Everest Freer write an opera about Pandora?

35. What was the real name of the American actress "Lotta"?

36. Where did Thomas W.F. Gann, the British archeologist, receive his early training?

37. Dave Garroway published and sold some book or pamphlet before he became famous. What was its title?

38. Can you locate the article about Kid Gavilan written by J. Lardner?

39. What statue by Johannes S. Gelert can be seen in Battle Creek, Michigan?

40. Who were some of the outstanding geographers in the U.S. in the 19th century?

41. Where was James Riddle Goffe born?

42. Were any famous Americans born in Greece?

43. Who designed the Hell Gate Bridge in New York?

44.   Find a portrait of Josiah G. Holland, first editor of *Scribner's Monthly*.

45.   Who were the U.S. senators from Illinois in 1850?

46.   Find a portrait of Burl Ives.

47.   What was the early life of Albert Sidney Johnston? Where can one find further biographical material about him?

48.   Locate an article on Alice Cunningham Fletcher, American ethnologist, which provides numerous citations to other biographical sources.

49.   Find a portrait of Jennifer Jones.

50.   What was the relationship of Mrs. Charles Kean, the actress, to Charles Tree?

51.   What can you find concerning Florence Kelley, who died in the 1930s?

52.   Where did William C. Kendall, the naturalist, receive his education?

53.   In what colleges did William P. Ker teach?

54.   Did Henry Churchill King wear glasses?

55.   How old was David Kinnison when he died?

56.   What famous Americans went to Knox College?

57.   For what was Leonard Knyff principally known?

58.   What Americans have received the Laetare Medal?

59.   Who was the first American manufacturer of the anvil?

60.   Who were some of the important librarians in the U.S. in the 19th century?

61. What were the highlights in the life of Francis J. Lippitt?

62. Can you find a portrait of Arthur Cushman McGiffert?

63. Where did Archibald MacLeish go to college?

64. What has been the career of General A.G.L. McNaughton of Canada?

65. What book designing has been done by Paul McPharlin?

66. Who is called "the father of American map making"?

67. Who was Juan Ruíz d'Alarcon y Mendoza?

68. Where was Anastas Mikoyan born?

69. What was the occupation of Leopold Seyffert, born in California in 1888?

70. Who was Allen G. Newman?

71. What was the business of John Howard Nodal's father?

72. How did the American singer Nordica happen to take this name?

73. When did Paul Ambrose Oliver die?

74. Who was Jacobus Oud?

75. Who was Secretary of War in Polk's administration?

76. Who was the first Bishop of the Protestant Episcopal Church in the U.S.?

77. Can you find a biographical sketch of Sir Walter A. Raleigh? Where can a picture of him be found?

78. Find a portrait of Gertrude Rand, the psychologist.

79.   What was Jacob Rayman's profession?

80.   Had Paul Robeson played Othello before 1944?

81.   How is the name Ruthven pronounced in Scotland?

82.   What was the career of John Drew Salmon?

83.   Who was president *pro tem* of the Senate of the U.S. in 1815?

84.   For what accomplishment is Nellie Ross remembered?

85.   When was C. Aubrey Smith knighted?

86.   What are the birth and death dates of Godfrey Thring?

87.   Locate a list of published works written by Margaret Truman.

88.   Were any famous Americans born in Turkey?

89.   Who was the first woman member of the clergy in the Unitarian
       Church?

90.   What was the original spelling of William Faulkner's surname?

91.   In what year did T.S. Eliot receive the Nobel prize for
       literature?

92.   Where was Thornton Wilder born?

93.   What famous Americans went to William and Mary College?

94.   What was the profession of Thomas Burks Yuille, who died in
       1934?

95.   Locate a lengthy, signed biography of President John Adams,
       with a bibliography of works about him.

96.   What is the address of the Soviet foreign trade official, Aziz
       Aga-Aga-bab Alekperov?

97.   Where could you find a scholarly article with a bibliography about Samuel Barron, the Confederate naval officer?

98.   In what sources can biographies of Pietro Cavallini be found?

99.   What is the title of Aleksandr Solzhenitsyn's autobiography?

100. Locate a portrait and autograph of David Crockett, the American who died defending the Alamo.

101. What is the correct pronunciation of John Donne's last name?

102. Find the birthplace of Isadora Duncan, the American-born dancer who died in 1927.

103. Who were the parents of the deceased U.S. corporation executive, Benjamin F. Fairless?

104. Find Dame Margot Fonteyne's birth date.

105. Who was the U.S. Ambassador to France in 1832?

106. What books has Frederick B. Gipson written besides *Old Yeller,* which has an appeal to children, and would it be possible to find his picture and an illustration from one of his books?

107. Who is Beverly Linney Hallam, an American, who has something to do with art?

108. Where could you find an article on Joseph Hebert, grandson of Canada's first settler?

109. Where could you find a list of reference books on Italian pseudonyms?

110. Where could one find a fairly long article on Amanda Theodosia Jones, an American inventor who died in 1914?

111. What essays have been written recently about D.H. Lawrence?

112. Find a list of American Nobel prize winners.

113.   Who was Thomas Love Peacock?

114.   What was the occupation of Horace H. Rackham, an American who lived between 1858 and 1933?

115.   What was the English painter Joseph Farington's subject specialty?

116.   Where could you find a signature facsimile of the American author Katharine Green Rohlfs?

117.   Find a list of biographical dictionaries in many languages dealing with people in library science and the book arts.

118.   Where could you find information concerning the background of the Canadian manufacturer William Ian Mackenzie Turner?

119.   What is the educational background of the American Charles Henry Watts II?

120.   Where can I find a lengthy, signed biography of William Wordsworth, which includes a list of portraits of the poet?

121.   Find an evaluative biography of the late British poet A.E. Housman.

122.   Locate an evaluative biography of the Puritan clergyman Cotton Mather.

123.   What was the birth date of the late British actor Ronald Colman?

124.   With which important event in American history is Robert Morris (1734-1806) associated?

125.   In what area of science were the Shull brothers active?

126.   Find an evaluative biography with a bibliography on Thomas Jefferson.

127. Who was the author of an article on Chaucer appearing in 1956?

128. In what source would you find a list of biographical dictionaries of women artists from the seventh century B.C. to 1970?

129. When did Bret Harte die?

130. How do you pronounce the name Abdullah?

131. What reference source would you consult to find out what Andrew Jackson's mother's maiden name was?

132. What is Frank Sinatra's address?

133. Find biographies of Swedenborgian ministers.

134. In what year was the Ethical Culture Society founded?

135. What is the date of death of Sir Gilbert Hollinshed Bloomfield Jackson, the late chairman of the Conscientious Objector Appellate Tribunal of England?

136. Where could you look to see if Sir Henry Head was really a neurologist and the editor of *Brain*?

137. What was Lenin's full name?

138. Locate a list of essays on Alexander Pope.

139. What was the education of Luis Muñoz Marín, a governor of Puerto Rico?

140. What is the date of birth of the late William Gibson, appointed Parliament Secretary in 1937?

141. Who was called the "father of the American cotton industry"?

142. Find the birthplace of John Stark.

143. Find dates for Samuel Allibone, lexicographer and librarian.

144.   Who was Louis Swift?

145.   What significant contribution did Sir Thomas Lombe (1685 - 1739) make to the textile industry?

146.   Where would you find information on Clarence's relationship to Richard III?

147.   Where would you look for the present address of Pierre Salinger?

148.   What was the Baron of Fairfield's real name?

149.   Where could you easily discover what Sir John Cope did to Bonnie Prince Charles?

150.   Where would you look if you wanted to know if John Ciardi, the American, has any sons?

151.   Locate a list of books by Lloyd Goodrich, the noted museum director.

152.   Where did David Hessler go to undergraduate school?

153.   What is the educational background of the Rev. Cuthbert Charles Lattey, the late British theologian?

154.   Who was the governor of Rhode Island in 1640?

155.   Find a brief statement of Charles Steinmetz's contribution to electrical engineering.

156.   Find a biography of Mary Ann Bickerdyke, a nurse during the Civil War.

157.   What businessmen have made the news recently?

158.   Locate a list of the important films directed by François Truffaut.

159.   What reference source would you consult to find out who John Lodge was?

160.   Who was Speaker of the House during Van Buren's administration?

161.   Where can the title of a dictionary of Polish poets be found?

162.   Where can be found a list of works by Euripides?

163.   How is the Chinese name Yung Cheng pronounced?

164.   Where can be found a biography of Gaius Lucilius, the Roman satirist?

165.   Where can be found a list of people historically associated with the Cape of Good Hope?

166.   Where can be found the name of the reigning king of Jordan?

167.   Locate a picture of Sean Connery.

168.   Find a list of businessmen currently in the news.

169.   Find a biography of Ian Smith.

170.   Locate a biography and picture of Richard Burton.

171.   Find a concise biography of Napoleon Bonaparte.

172.   Find the title of a novel written by Giorgio de Chirico, an Italian artist who influenced the surrealists.

173.   Locate references to current periodical articles on J.S. Bach.

174.   Find a reference to an obituary of Robert Frost.

175.   Find a list of essays about Marcel Proust.

176.   Find a reference to a critical essay about Sinclair Lewis's *Elmer Gantry*.

177. Find a citation to a biography of Virginia Dare, the first child of English parents born in the New World.

178. Find a critical appraisal of Dostoievski's *Crime and Punishment*.

179. Find a biography of Andrew Jackson appropriate for a child.

180. Where is Robert Morris, the American Revolutionary War financier, buried?

181. Find a biography of Ernest Hemingway.

182. Locate a list of past presidents of the University of Chicago.

183. Find a list of the major publications of the anthropologist, Ruth Benedict, who lived from 1887 to 1948.

184. What was the educational background of the entertainer Jean Harlow?

185. What pseudonyms has Marjorie Prebble used?

186. Does Luis Zalamea have any children?

187. What awards has David G. Simons received?

188. Find a picture of Andre Norton, a writer of science fiction.

189. What were the political activities of Benjamin Franklin?

190. When did King George III die?

191. What was Woodrow Wilson's occupation before he became president?

192. Who are some of the famous people in American history who were born in Indiana?

193. What was Millard Fillmore's birth date?

194. Find a biography of F. Scott Fitzgerald with a portrait.

195. Find a list of women abolitionists.

196. Find an evaluation of Miles Standish.

197. Locate a description of the childhood of Henry VIII.

198. What was Charles Marriott's profession?

199. When was Major Edward Fagan, the late English military officer, born?

200. When was Lloyd George, the former prime minister of England, born?

201. Find an evaluative biography of Oliver Cromwell.

202. Where was Howard Hughes born?

203. Find a lengthy biography of James McNeill Whistler.

204. What was the death date of Aubrey Beardsley, the English artist?

205. What is the pronunciation of Fa-Hsien, the fourth-century Chinese priest and author?

206. Find a discussion of the career of Rabbi Stephen Wise, an early twentieth-century religious leader.

207. Find a biography and a listing of works of Alexander Pope.

208. Locate recent periodical articles on Beethoven.

209. Find the birth and death dates of the American evangelist, Aimee Semple McPherson.

210. Find a biography with a portrait of Soupy Sales.

211.   Find an account of the projects initiated by Louise Caldwell
        Murdock, founder of the Twentieth Century Club of Wichita,
        Kansas in 1896.

212.   Find a biography, with a picture, of Carolyn Keene, the author
        of the Nancy Drew books.

213.   Locate an evaluative biography of Peter Roget, a nineteenth-
        century London physician.

214.   Find a biography with a photograph of Neil Armstrong, the
        astronaut.

215.   Find a list of books in which can be found biographical articles
        about Borodin, a nineteenth-century Russian composer.

216.   In what magazine did an article about Charles Dickens called
        "Dip into Dickens" appear in 1962?

217.   Find career information on the late Sir J. William Dawson,
        former Principal of McGill University in Montreal.

218.   What did Enoch Lincoln, who lived from 1788 to 1892, do in
        American history?

219.   Find a biography of Enrico Dandolo, who lived from 1108 to
        1205.

220.   Find a biography of Joseph Kennedy.

221.   Find a short biography of Ralph W. Gallagher, former
        Chairman of Standard Oil, who died in 1952.

222.   How is the last name of John Gielgud pronounced?

223.   Find a list of Italian biographical dictionaries.

224.   Who was Coriolanus?

225.   What was the date of death of Frederick Stock?

226. For what poem is the twelfth-century poet Owain Cyveiliog famous?

227. How is Christopher Columbus's name spelled in Spanish and Italian?

228. Find a list of materials on T.S. Eliot.

229. How is "Pulitzer" pronounced?

230. What was the birthplace of Will Carleton?

231. What was the first name of Mr. Oswald, who was sent to Paris to ascertain the nature of American peace terms in 1782?

232. Find a biography of Loretta Young.

233. Find the title of a biography of W. Hogarth.

234. Find a scholarly, signed article, with a bibliography on Caleb Harris, a nineteenth-century American bibliophile.

235. Find a list of U.S. senators from 1789 to 1937.

236. Find a biography of the American architect, Samuel Inman Cooper.

237. Find a summary of the stage career of Robert Newton, the English actor who died in 1956.

238. Find the title of a periodical article published in 1974 about the marriage of King Charles II of England.

239. Find a signed article on Sir Richard Whitbourne, the sixteenth-century English adventurer.

240. Find an evaluative biography of James Tanner, a deceased American lobbyist.

241. Locate an article on the founder of Detroit.

242.   Find an international list of biographical dictionaries of musicians.

243.   Find a biography of Louis Untermeyer.

244.   In which encyclopedias would I find articles about Jay Gould, who lived from 1836 to 1892?

245.   Find a biography of Adolph Ochs, publisher of the *New York Times* from 1896 to 1935, with the correct pronunciation of his name.

246.   Where did Robert E. Beard receive the Ph.D. in Slavic linguistics?

247.   Where may I find a biography of the actress Patricia Neal?

248.   Find a brief biography of Elvis Presley.

249.   I just finished reading *Delta Wedding* by Eudora Welty and I sure would like to know more about her, where can I look?

250.   What qualities of Meriwhether Lewis made him a good candidate for exploration of uncharted lands?

251.   What is Cher's real name?

252.   Where would I find a picture of Midori, the violinist?

253.   Where could I find a biography of Alice Kroger, librarian?

254.   Who is Kawabata Yasunari?

255.   Where can I find magazine articles that cover the conflicts of Michael Jackson and his brothers precluding their Victory Tour?

256.   What awards in librarianship has Frederick Gridley Kilgour received?

257.   What famous person was Albert Einstein describing when he said that he/she was "of all celebrated beings, the only one whom fame has not corrupted"?

258.   I'd like to know the political affiliation and home address of M. Margaret McKeown.

259.   Where was Kurt Vonnegut educated?

260.   At what address could the British conductor Sir Neville Marriner be reached?

261.   I want to find out what elected positions Diane Feinstein has held.

262.   Where can I find a list of the reigning royal family of Liechtenstein?

263.   Is Anthony Andrews married? And where can I write to him?

264.   I want to find personal, in-depth information on Anita Roddick, British businesswoman and social activist.

265.   Exactly who was Lizzie Borden, and what is all the hub-bub about?

266.   From what Native American language does the word "Michigan" derive, and what does it mean?

267.   Where can I find extensive biographical information about the popular singer Paula Abdul which would include comments from her and from people who know her?

268.   I want to find some background information on the writer A.S. Byatt. She won the Booker Prize in 1990. Where should I look?

269.   Did Nkenge Zola go to college in Michigan?

270.   Who are the reigning rulers of the United Arab Emirates, and when did they come into power?

271.   What are Peter Greenaway's latest projects?

272.   When was Johann Sebastian Bach born and when did he die?

273.   I just read a book about Vita Sackville-West and I would like to find out more about her. Can you help me?

274.   I found an old photograph in my attic of a man dressed in a U.S. military uniform. The photograph is signed "Benjamin Cheever." How can I discover whether Benjamin Cheever was anyone of importance in history and whether the man in the picture is actually Benjamin Cheever?

275.   Who was Alfred Nobel?

276.   I'd like to know something about Scott Turow, who wrote *Presumed Innocent*. Is he a lawyer?

277.   What was Frederick Graff's most notable achievement in Philadelphia?

278.   I am a big fan of Phil Collins and I was wondering where I could look to find a picture of him and his address?

279.   I need an introduction to the life of the late American sculptor, Harriet Hosmer.

280.   I am looking for information about an ancestor. His name was Rittenhouse Neisser. He was a minister, a teacher at a seminary, and a librarian. I know he died in 1949.

281.   When was Nestor Jost a member of the Legislative Assembly of Rio Grande do Sul?

282.   I just love the actress Laura Dern and want to learn more about her. Would there be anything about her in the library?

283.   When was Francis Ford Coppola born?

284.   At what address can I write to Akira Kurosawa?

285. Can you tell me anything about author Sue Grafton?

286. How many children does the famous Gerald Bentley currently
      have?

287. Where might you find a picture of and biographical information
      about the popular cartoonist Gary Larson?

288. My Latin textbook (it's published in England) quotes a little
      rhyme about "I do not love thee, Dr. Fell." Who was Dr. Fell?

Reference Materials

African American Biographies
American Men and Women of Science
Biographical Dictionaries and Related Works
Biographical Dictionary of Black Americans
Biography and Genealogy Master Index
Biography Index
Canadian Who's Who
Chambers's Biographical Dictionary
Contemporary Authors
Contemporary Black Biography
Current Biography
Dictionary of American Biography
Dictionary of Canadian Biography
Dictionary of National Biography
Dictionary of Universal Biography
Directory of American Scholars
Encyclopedia of American Biography
Essay and General Literature Index
Historical Biographical Dictionaries Master Index
Index to Women of the World
International Who's Who
McGraw-Hill Encyclopedia of World Biography
National Cyclopedia of American Biography
New York Times Biographical Service
Notable American Women

Notable Americans
Notable Black American Women
Notable Names in American History
Personal Name Index to the New York Times Index
Something About the Author
Webster's American Biographies
Webster's Biographical Dictionary
Webster's New Biographical Dictionary
Who Was Who
Who Was Who in America
Who Was Who in America. Historical Volume
Who's Who
Who's Who Among Black Americans
Who's Who in America
Who's Who in the World
Who's Who of American Women

CHAPTER 5

BIBLIOGRAPHY

Reference Interviews

Patron #1.   A man.

Patron: Do you have a list of Andrew Lang's colored books?
Librarian: Did you want just those in print now?
Patron: Yes.

Where would you look?

Patron #2.   A high school girl.

Patron: I'd like to find out the definition of "bolt."
Librarian: Did you check our unabridged dictionary?
Patron: No—but this has to do with books. I think it might be a part of a book.

Where would you find book trade terms?

Patron #3.   A woman.

Patron: How do I find out if a book is still in print?
Librarian: What information do you have about the book —author, title?
Patron: It's *The Spy* by James Fenimore Cooper.

Where could you find this information?

Patron #4.   A young woman.

Patron:	I want to know if this book, *Rape of the Fair Country,* is still in print and who the publisher is now. It's British. I've already checked *Books in Print* and it's not there.
Librarian:	Who is the author?
Patron:	Alexander Cordell.
Librarian:	According to *CBI* Alexander Cordell is a pseudonym.

Where would you go now?

Patron #5.   A man.

Patron:	I really have a problem and I don't think you can help me but you're my last resort.
Librarian:	What's the problem?
Patron:	My wife saw a book a few months ago that she said she wanted. I'd like to order it for her for Christmas, but I can't remember the author or title.
Librarian:	Do you know what the book is about?
Patron:	Yes, it's an art book.
Librarian:	Do you know if it was about the art of a certain period or country?
Patron:	Well, I think it was about the history of Mexican art and as I remember, it was quite expensive—around $25 or $30.

Where would you check?

Patron #6.   A high school student.

Patron:	I need some books of historical fiction.
Librarian:	Historical fiction of what country?
Patron:	United States.
Librarian:	Any particular period?
Patron:	Around the Revolutionary War.

Where could you find a list of suitable novels?

Patron #7.   A woman.

Patron:	I'm interested in the poems of Phillis Wheatley.
Librarian:	You'd like to read some of her poems?
Patron:	Yes.
Librarian:	*Granger's Index of Poetry* only lists four of her poems. We might have one or two of them in an anthology; or did you want an entire book of her poems?
Patron:	I'd prefer a book if there is one.

Where would you look?

Patron #8.   A woman.

Patron:	I would like to see a list of fiction books.
Librarian:	There is a list of current best-sellers at the check-out desk. Is that what you want?
Patron:	No, I'd like a longer list, maybe with some critical remarks.

Where would you look?

Patron #9.   A man.

Patron:	I'd like to find out something about Oriental games— Japanese or Chinese chess.
Librarian:	(Looking in *Subject Guide to BIP*) There are two listed here.
Patron:	I wanted to buy one or two books, so I'd prefer something in paperback.

Where would you go?

Patron #10.   A high school boy.

Patron:	Do you have any war stories?
Librarian:	About any special war?
Patron:	Yes, World War II.
Librarian:	Are you interested in fiction or non-fiction?
Patron:	Fiction.

Where would you check?

Reference Questions

1. How would you locate a library within the U.S. which has a special collection on Beethoven? Where is it?

2. Explain what is meant by a "Bowdlerized text."

3. Who publishes an in-print English-Vietnamese dictionary?

4. Does Allen Ginsberg have a collection of poems available in paperback?

5. Define the following abbreviations from the book trade: ABA, Bds, Col (d), P.P., T.L.s.

6. Find a definition of "corner clip." What is the Spanish equivalent of this term?

7. What is the translation of "proofreading" into Spanish?

8. What do the initials I.D.P. stand for?

9. Find three phono records of Irish folk dance music.

10. Find three books for a 5th grader who wants to learn about puppetry.

11. Is LC the only library which holds *American New Life*, v. 1-, 1901-?

12. Who published Joe Louis's autobiography?

13. What is the title of a work by John Champneys printed in London in 1548?

14. What U.S. libraries hold the Institute of Makers of Explosives pamphlet no. 17, 1960?

15. Where could one find an annotated list of books about U.S. foreign policy which are recommended for high school students?

16. Which library has a master microfilm of John Wesley's *A Short English Grammar*?

17. What does the term "agate," which is used in connection with book binding, mean?

18. What U.S. library has a copy of David Raymond Cheney's *Animals in a Midsummer Night's Dream,* which was written in 1955?

19. What is the address of the Antiquarian Bookseller's Association?

20. Find the French and Spanish terms for "bookworm."

21. What are some synonyms for "half-title" as used in library science?

22. What is the title of a book on chess suitable for children?

23. Where could one find the names of some pamphlets on Yugoslavia?

24. What is the title of the book that Margaret Truman Daniels wrote in 1969?

25. What did Lady Marie Thérèse Louise Dickens publish in 1936?

26. Can you suggest an in-print book on "Family Allowances"?

27. Who has been called the "father of modern painting"?

28. What are the titles of some books on the floral arts which are appropriate for a public library?

29. What does the Czech word "bukinista," mean?

30. What are some of the more significant recent developments in the area of information science?

31. What is the title of the book Marion Levy wrote on China in 1949?

32. Find an article on libraries in Afghanistan.

33. Find recent statistics on the educational status of library users in the U.S.

34. Find a few paragraphs defining the term, "limited edition."

35. Find a bibliography of Iris Murdoch's works along with a short, critical biography of her and a list of works about her.

36. Who is the law librarian for the New Mexico Supreme Court?

37. Who really wrote "How I won over fifty prizes in weekly periodicals," a work originally signed with the initials "J. E. S."?

38. How would you say "reference department" in six languages?

39. Has anyone published a bibliography of graduate theses and dissertations about the American Indian?

40. Who wrote *Analysis of the Game of Chess,* published in London in 1819?

41. What is the French equivalent for the term "short title"?

42. Has anyone published a bibliography of the works of Adam Smith?

43. Find an excerpt from a review of Edna Ferber's book *So Big* .

44. Which special libraries are located in Princeton, New Jersey?

45. What is the mailing address of the librarian Elizabeth Stone?

46. What is the Library of Congress number of *Time as Dimension and History* by Hubert Griggs Alexander, published by the University of Mexico Press in 1945?

47. What does the Swedish word "bibliografisk" mean ?

48. How would one say "xerography" in Bulgarian?

49. What is the book budget at the University of Alaska Library?

50. What is the name of a Venezuelan bibliography on education?

51. What is the educational background of the librarian Robert Coale?

52. Locate the real author of *Mabel* written under the pseudonym Grace Ramsay.

53. Find the approximate value of a first edition of Dickens's *Mystery of Edwin Drood*.

54. What is the meaning of the Italian term "pagine"?

55. What are the titles of some recent bibliographies published on the subject of demography?

56. What are the correct uses of italics in preparing a work for printing?

57. What are some books on the subject of kindergarten?

58. I have just received the proofs for my book from the publisher. What do I do with them now?

59. What other work has the author of *Discipline,* published in Edinburgh in 1814, written?

60. If someone described a book to you as "grossissimo," where would you find out what that means?

61.   What doctoral dissertation has been written on the novels of Robert Bage?

62.   I have a new job as a proofreader for the college paper. What will be some of my responsibilities?

63.   Where would one find out the meaning of "elite type"?

64.   What are the anonymous publications of President James Madison?

65.   Where may I find a copy of the letter written by Columbus after he discovered America?

66.   Where might one find out whether or not the New York Times Photo Library is open to the public?

67.   Is there a library in the U.S. where I can find some special material on the Mennonites?

68.   How many degrees were awarded in library science last year?

69.   Under what two pseudonyms did Eliza Louisa Moresby Beck publish her novel and short stories in the 1930s?

70.   List the single works of Rudyard Kipling.

71.   Where might one go to find out what is on the other side of a recording by William Primrose of Hindemith's *Der Schwanendreher* issued with the L.C. card #R54-812?

72.   Where can I find a list of books on twentieth-century music?

73.   Where might one find the name of the head librarian of the Vermont Historical Society Library?

74.   Where could one find the title of a book to study to prepare for the Civil Service Exam for elevator inspectors?

75.   How many new books were published in the field of fiction in the U.S. last year?

76. Where might one find a list of books on communism in the U.S. for which L.C. cards were issued last year?

77. Where might one go to find a list of Bulgarian fiction books that were assigned L.C. cards last year?

78. Where might one find the imprint of the original printing of Walt Whitman's *November Boughs*?

79. What are some good books suggesting chemical experiments for third grade children?

80. Which auction house sold a first edition of R.L. Stevenson's *Child's Garden of Verses* in 1895?

81. Is there a book written about the first ladies of the U.S.?

82. What would be some good books to use as the nucleus of a new undergraduate library?

83. Was *Treasure Island* sold in first edition in 1894 at an American auction?

84. Where would one find the name of the publisher and cost of the book *Chitty-chitty-bang-bang* by Ian Fleming?

85. Locate the titles of several currently published books dealing with African writers.

86. What does the word "stereotype" mean in its original sense? It has something to do with printing.

87. Where would you find recent dissertations in the field of literature?

88. Where might one find a list of libraries in the country that have Charles Guthrie's book, *Blood Vessel Surgery and Its Applications* (1959)?

89. Locate the titles of some current dictionaries dealing with cookery.

90. Where would one find the birth date of the famous bookman, Elmer Adler?

91. What are the names of some libraries in Oslo, Norway?

92. Where might one find the Library of Congress number for *Middlesex*, a 1951 book by Norman Brett-James?

93. Where can I find an account of English book illustration in the early 1900s, written by a contemporary of the period?

94. Which publishers are still printing copies of William Faulkner's *Light in August*? Are any paperback editions currently available?

95. What price was paid in 1895 for an autographed letter signed by Charles Baudelaire to his publisher in which Victor Hugo and Théophile Gautier were mentioned?

96. Is there an English translation of Sartre's play *Les Sèquestres d'Altona*?

97. Where might one find out the size of a book called *Who's to Blame* by Henry Fauntleroy, printed in 1883?

98. Where would one go to find fairly complete reproductions of L.C. cards if one were preparing a bibliography in the field of organic chemistry?

99. Where might one find a number of books on antibiotics published recently?

100. What kind of book activities are carried on by the Agency for International Development?

101. Is there a library in New York that has a special collection on Mary, Queen of Scots?

102. Where can one find the meaning of the abbreviation "cf.," a term used in a footnote or bibliography?

103.   Who is the author of *Adventures of an Irish Gentleman*, published anonymously in London in 1830?

104.   Where might one find the L.C. card number for a set of the complete works of Brahms printed by J.W. Edwards in 1949?

105.   Are any editions of the *Holy Quran* currently available which provide both the Arabic text and an English translation?

106.   Who were the authors of an 1899 British work on hockey?

107.   Locate information regarding current developments concerning the Copyright Office of the Library of Congress for the previous year.

108.   Locate the translation of the French word "rayonnage" into English.

109.   What is the German word for "foliated"?

110.   What is "oversewing"?

111.   What are the dimensions of a sextodecimo edition?

112.   What is the difference between the words "serials" and "series"?

113.   Locate information on John Baskerville, the English printer.

114.   Does the University of Alberta Press have a book in print on the history of Boeotia?

115.   What is the meaning of "rubricated"?

116.   What is the meaning of "offprint"?

117.   What are "incunabula"?

118.   For what does "C. & P." stand?

119.   Identify the term "Chiswick Press."

120.   Find an explanation of MARC tapes, which are used by many libraries.

121.   What is "flexible classification"?

122.   What is the meaning of the Dutch book term "vellen"?

123.   Who was Pierre Simon Fournier?

124.   How is "publisher's catalog" translated into German?

125.   Locate a list of publications of the American Society for Information Science for the previous year.

126.   How many bibliographies on St. John Chrysostom have been prepared by Dom Baur?

127.   What does the proofreading mark "#" mean?

128.   Find rules for the use of italics in printing.

129.   Locate a list of works distinguished as the "Best Children's Books" of the previous year. How are these books selected and by what group?

130.   Have any libraries in the Decatur, Illinois area been designated as U.S. government depositories?

131.   What type of bookmobile services are offered by the Toronto Public Library (Canada)?

132.   How does one make footnote references to legal documents?

133.   What is the format for compiling a list of tables to be included in a dissertation?

134.   Locate rules for dividing words at the ends of lines.

135.   How does one make a bibliography of illustrations?

136.   Which colleges and universities in New York offer graduate programs in library science?

137.   What is the correct right-hand margin to be used in typing a thesis?

138.   Find the name of a bibliography of Coptic literature printed in Russian.

139.   Find a bibliography about Japanese theater and drama.

140.   Find a reference to a recent bibliography listing military books.

141.   Locate recent bibliographies about information storage and retrieval systems.

142.   Find the title of a Dutch bibliography of Javanese literature.

143.   Find the condition and approximate value of a map of Mexico by J. Hutawa, produced in 1863.

144.   Which auction house sold a 1696 Dutch translation of *Don Quixote*?

145.   What was the auction price, at the most recent sale, of a first edition of Blackstone's *Commentaries on the Laws of England*?

146.   Find a list of books of ghost stories for children.

147.   Have any of Yukio Misima's works been translated into English?

148.   What is Kate Norway's real name?

149.   Where may be found information on discounts from publishers to book stores?

150.   Are there any books in print about Adolf Eichmann, the late Nazi?

151.   Are any of B.F. Skinner's books available in paper bindings?

152.   What significance does the term "diaper" have for the book
       trade and library profession?

153.   What is a more common term for "duodecimo"?

154.   How many sheets does a ream of paper contain and how would
       you communicate the answer to a German-speaking person?

155.   For what specialized bookbinding techniques is the Edwards
       family of Halifax remembered?

156.   What is the correct format for citing congressional bills and
       resolutions before they have been enacted?

157.   Find a brief account of the library system of a state prison in
       Denmark.

158.   From which institution can a microfilmed copy of the *Book of
       Mormon* be obtained?

159.   Is *Putnam's Magazine* available in microform?

160.   How much does *Gone with the Wind* cost in paperback?

161.   Find a brief description of the New England Document
       Conservation Center.

162.   Who publishes *Fraser's Canadian Trade Directory* in Canada?

163.   Where is the master microform from which copies of Lang's
       Modern Mythology may be ordered?

164.   Locate a table giving the recommended metric sizes for books.

165.   How much does a copy of *The Adventures of Pinocchio* cost?

166.   Where could one find the title of a thesis written on the
       Brontës?

167.   Where could one find a list of pamphlets on drug abuse?

168. Where could one find an annotated list of travel guides to foreign countries?

169. Did the *Library Journal give* Heyerdahl's *Aku-Aku* a favorable review?

170. Find a synopsis of Robert Bolt's play *A Man for All Seasons.*

171. Find a list of atlases and maps useful in a public library.

172. Locate the title of a good book about ballet for fifth grade children.

173. In which anthologies can a fairy tale entitled "The Jolly Tailor Who Became King" be located?

174. What are some synonymous terms for "variorum edition" used by U.S. publishers?

175. Find a list of psychological novels.

176. Who was the original publisher of J.R.R. Tolkien's *Lord of the Rings* trilogy?

177. Is Victoria Holt's novel *The Legend of the Seventh Virgin,* suitable for teenagers?

178. What are some good college level books in the field of plant physiology?

179. Who published Bertolt Brecht's *Mutter Courage und Ihre Kinder* ?

180. Find a brief biographical sketch of Dante Gabriel Rossetti, the Italian poet.

181. How much does John Berryman's *77 Dream Songs* cost and which publisher puts it out?

182. Which editions of Shakespeare's works are available in paperback?

183.   Find an annotated, evaluative list of books on word usage.

184.   Is John Kenneth Galbraith's *Economic Development in Perspective* recommended for public libraries?

185.   Find the full order information and quotations from critics on *Waiting for Godot* by Samuel Beckett.

186.   Find a list of biographies about black people suitable for teenagers.

187.   Would *Veronica's Smile* by Roger Duvoisin or *A Dog So Small* by Philippa Pearce be better for a six-year-old?

188.   From where could a pamphlet on venereal disease be ordered?

189.   What are the nicknames of Martin Bormann, the German Nazi party leader?

190.   What do the initials stand for in J.R.R. Tolkien's name?

191.   Who was the first American black novelist?

192.   Should the "S" in Harry S Truman's name have a period after it?

193.   Find a list of articles written in the first decade of this century about librarianship as a career for women.

194.   Find summaries of recent works on the application of computers to librarianship.

195.   Find evaluative remarks on recent books in the field of information science.

196.   Locate a summary account of the damage sustained by libraries in Florence during the November 1966 floods.

197.   Find an illustrated article on ancient libraries.

198. Locate a biographical sketch of Vasilii Anastasevich, an early nineteenth-century Russian.

199. What is the name of the librarian at the University of Toronto?

200. A doctoral student in English literature is writing a dissertation on Herman Melville. Which library in the U.S. has the most comprehensive collection of materials by and about this author suitable for an exhaustive study?

201. What is the pseudonym of Alfred du Pont?

202. Locate the address of your state library association.

203. Find a list of associations especially interested in the automation of libraries.

204. Find a list of officers of the Canadian Library Association.

205. What is the total public library circulation for Illinois?

206. What are the locations of U.S.I.A. libraries in Europe?

207. How many volumes are in the New York Public Library?

208. What types of special materials on Frank Lloyd Wright does the Northwestern University Library have in its collection?

209. In which New York serial was Nathaniel Hawthorne's story "The Snow Image" first published?

210. Where could one find a bibliography of the works of Jonathan Edwards?

211. Where could one find the title of an unpublished thesis by Albert Díaz about the Latin American collection in the University of North Carolina library?

212. What kinds of material on music history are to be found in the Detroit Public Library's Music and Performing Arts Department?

213. Locate a list of libraries which have special collections of rare books.

214. Was there ever an edition published of *The Castle* by Franz Kafka which contained an introduction by Thomas Mann?

215. Find the address of the General Electric Company Computer Department Library.

216. What are some of the special collections of the J.M. Longyear Research Library of the Marquette County (Michigan) Historical Society?

217. What is the size of the Kimball Public Library in Randolph, Vermont?

218. Find a list of the early editions and manuscripts of Thomas Paine held in the Clements Library of the University of Michigan.

219. Find a list of U.S. regional libraries for the blind.

220. What are requirements for membership in the American Theological Library Association?

221. Find a bibliographical description of an 1872 edition of Thomas Hardy's book, *Under the Greenwood Tree*.

222. Find full bibliographical information for *The National Guardsman,* a journal published from 1877 to 1878.

223. Find full bibliographical information for a book published in 1941 by a man named Otto Gliss.

224. What did Edith Abbott Fritten, who died in 1957, write in her lifetime?

225. Find bibliographical information on a map of Capitola, California, printed in 1949.

226. Find bibliographical information about the libretto of *Camelot*, a musical comedy copyrighted in 1961.

227.   Find a listing of children's books about medicine.

228.   Who translated an 1817 edition of the complete Bible into Chinese?

229.   Who was the publisher of an edition of Dante's *The Purgatorio* which provided an Italian and English version on opposite pages?

230.   Did the Library of Congress catalog any books about the Hittite language from July through September, 1967?

231.   Who was the publisher of Benjamin Musser's *Bucolics and Caviar,* which came out in 1930?

232.   Find the Library of Congress number, the translator, and a list of libraries holding a copy of Natalia Ginzburg's *A Light for Fools,* published in 1956.

233.   Locate a list of Christmas stories available on filmstrips.

234.   Has the Library of Congress cataloged any of the Beatles' albums?

235.   Are there any American libraries which have copies of Claude Amiette's *Peine Perdue,* which was published in 1955?

236.   During which years was *La Revue Blanche,* a Parisian periodical, published?

237.   Find a list of critical and biographical works about the Marquis de Sade written in several different languages.

238.   From which source can one order copies printed from a master microfilm of the *New Jersey Journal of Pharmacy*?

239.   Are there any paperback books about computer-assisted instruction for sale?

240.   Find the name of one of the French-to-English translations of a Georges Simenon novel published outside the U.S.

241.   Who was the author of the anonymous play *The Macaroni* which was first presented in 1773 in York, England?

242.   Find a summary of a 1968 doctoral thesis on the Han dynasty in China.

243.   Find a list of separately collated bibliographies on children's literature with an international scope.

244.   Find a title of a 1967 bibliography on Victorian jewelry.

245.   What call number was assigned to *Peter Prim's Story Book* by the Library of Congress?

246.   Is *The Red Badge of Courage* available in a large type edition?

247.   Locate a list of good books about reptiles for high school students.

248.   Find a book about the Chinese language which is suitable for an elementary school child.

249.   Which record company has a 1968 recording of Puccini's *La Bohème*?

250.   Find the average price of a book published last year.

251.   What is the name of the director of the University of North Carolina libraries?

252.   Find the auction price of *Ballad Books*, edited by C.K. Sharpe and published in 1823.

253.   What is the meaning of the term "herdrukt" discovered in a Dutch bibliography?

254.   What is a "library edition"?

255.   If one needed a copy of Cornelius Baldwin's *Ancient Burial Cists in Northern Ohio*, which was published in 1882, where is the closest library holding a copy?

256. Does the University of Minnesota Press have any titles on home economics for sale?

257. Find annotations for children's books written by David C. Cooke.

258. What is the German equivalent of the English term, "classified arrangement"?

259. Find a list of the books about Musa Kaago which have been published in English in the twentieth century.

260. What does "unlettered" mean to the antiquarian bookman?

261. Find a list of paperback books about Franklin D. Roosevelt.

262. Find a summary of Sidney Mitchell's 1963 doctoral thesis on Joseph Conrad.

263. Find an explanation of an extension card in library practice.

264. Were there any French bibliographies on the topic of hypnotism published before 1900?

265. Locate an essay on the history of French literature which includes a bibliography listing the current prices of the books.

266. What awards has Carl Sandburg received?

267. Which libraries have the *Baltimore Philosophical Journal* on microfilm?

268. What is the address of the publisher of the *Book of Knowledge* ?

269. What is the address of the Barrows Publishing Company?

270. What are the titles of some novels about New York City?

271. What is the address of Scribner's?

272. What is the address of the publisher Stratford House?

273.   What is the address of McGraw-Hill?

274.   What is the title of a novel about music or musicians?

275.   What is the address of Funk and Wagnalls?

276.   Find a list of books on Napoleon.

277.   Find a list of books on pyrometers.

278.   Locate a list of novels about early English history.

279.   Are there any novels about Valley Forge?

280.   Can you recommend a good novel about the Civil War in the U.S.?

281.   Are there any novels about the wives of Henry VIII?

282.   Are there any novels about South Africa?

283.   What are the names of special libraries in Alabama having Civil War collections?

284.   Who is the director of libraries at Case Western Reserve University?

285.   What is the price of the *Reader's Encyclopedia*?

286.   Find a list of books on ballet.

287.   What is a book scout?

288.   When did John Bell, the English bookseller, printer, and publisher live?

289.   What were the major activities of the Catholic Library Association last year?

290.   What does the Czech phrase "osli ucho," having to do with books, mean?

291. What is a "double entry" in library work?

292. What are the correct uses of italics in preparing a work for printing?

293. What did a first edition of Rudyard Kipling's *Just So Stories for Little Children* sell for in London in 1964?

294. In what periodical did Hattie M. Knight's article, "Library Education: A More Excellent Way," appear in the fall of 1969?

295. What books on the subject of lizards are currently for sale in the U.S.?

296. What special libraries are located in New Brunswick, New Jersey?

297. Who is the author of the novel, *At Home,* which on the title page says that it is by the "author of *English Fashionables Abroad*"?

298. What book by John D. Ryder did the Library of Congress acquire in 1949?

299. What is the punctuation mark "…" called and what is the Russian equivalent?

300. Locate a list of biographies of George Washington, with annotations, suitable for children and recommended by the American Library Association.

301. Find a list of microfilm masters, with libraries which hold them, for the works of Washington Irving.

302. Which U.S. libraries have copies of James Thomas Field's *Good Company for Every Day in the Year,* published in 1866?

303. Has the city of Adlington in Lancashire, England, published an official city guide since 1956?

304. What is a "llyfrigellyd"?

305. What children's books are available for sale on the subject of monsters?

306. What are the titles in the series *Concise Medical Textbooks*?

307. What is the price of *Les Misérables* by Victor Hugo, for use as a textbook in a secondary school?

308. What was the native country of Maria Augusta Trapp?

309. What was George Orwell's real name?

310. What is the address of the Nepal National Library?

311. Is there an edition of *Odessa File* by Frederick Forsyth available in a format appropriate for the visually handicapped?

312. What is the address of the Brazilian Association of Librarians?

313. For what does BCM stand?

314. I need some help with some computer terms for an exam. Where can I find some definitions of terms like "RAM," "cache" and "buffer"?

315. What is the correct form for citing a newspaper article?

316. What is the preferred style source in the biological sciences?

317. Where could I find a detailed description of how to edit a manuscript?

318. What does the word "bus" mean as a computer term?

319. This book is such an odd size; how should I properly describe this for our rare book collection catalog?

320. What does the Dutch word "overzetting" mean?

321. What does the Polish word "kolajonowany" mean?

322. I'm writing my dissertation and I need to know how to format my bibliography and footnotes.

323. What is an "object-oriented database"?

324. Where could a complete list of the recordings of Louis Armstrong be found?

325. Where can I find a list of ALA accredited library schools?

326. A friend of mine said he had a book covered with "ooze leather." I didn't want to display my lack of knowledge of the book trade so I didn't ask him what "ooze leather" was. Could you help me find a definition?

327. Is Hillsdale Public Library automated yet? And how much would I make if I worked there?

328. Where can I find a brief history of the Microsoft Corporation including a photograph of its founders?

329. I'm a little embarrassed. I still can't figure out where to put the punctuation when there are quotation marks at the end of a sentence. Can you help me out?

330. I have an 1843 edition of Charles Dickens's *A Christmas Carol*, what is it worth?

331. Where would I find a definition of the library terminology "mixed responsibility"?

332. Where and when was the ALA conference held in 1922 and how many people attended?

333. My math teacher told us our next assignment will use the Monte Carlo Method, but we don't know what that means.

334. Are there any books on religions from the Afro-American perspective?

335. Who publishes the CD-ROM of *Grimm's Fairy Tales*?

336.   I'm writing my doctoral dissertation on the mating behavior of red house finches and need to know if any other dissertations have been written about this vital topic?

337.   I have a take-home test and one of the questions asks, "What is a buffer." We've never talked about buffers in class and I can't find that term anywhere in our reading. Can you tell me where I might find a definition?

338.   Where can I find a bibliography of the works of Robert Louis Stevenson?

339.   What are some useful commentaries for a layman interested in Bible study?

340.   What does ASCII stand for?

341.   Where would I go to find out what the roman numeral DCC is?

342.   How could I find contemporary Yugoslavian (that was) authors and if any of their works are available in translation?

343.   What is "gampi"?

344.   I'm compiling a list of books written about partridges, and want to know if one has already been made, could you help me find out?

345.   What is *papel avitelado*?

346.   What format do I follow for this manuscript I'm preparing?

347.   I am interested in Modern American Poetry, can you suggest a reading list?

348.   Where can I find a book that will give me authors who have written about the Rio de la Plata?

349.   Where would you find current information (like brief descriptions, system requirements, and prices) on clip art software for CD-ROMs?

350.   I need to write a pamphlet about AIDS for high school students
        and I want to get some samples of what other people have done.

Reference Materials

ABC for Book Collectors
Acronyms and Abbreviations in Library and Information Work
A.L.A. Glossary of Library and Information Science
A.L.A. Membership Directory
American Book-Prices Current
American Book Publishing Record
American Library Directory
American Library Resources
American Library Resources. Supplements
American National Standards for Bibliographic References
Annual Review of Information Science and Technology
ANU SocSci Netlore
Applications Navigator
Archie File Index
Associations' Publications in Print
A-V Online
Best Books for Children
Best Books for Junior High Readers
Best Books for Senior High Readers
Best Videos for Children and Young Adults
Bibliographic Index
Bibliography of Library Economy
Black Access - A Bibliography of Afro-American Bibliographies
The Book of Video Lists
Bookman's Glossary
Bookman's Price Index
Books for College Libraries
Books in Print
Books in Series
Bowker Annual of Library and Book Trade Information
British Books in Print
British Museum. General Catalogue of Printed Books
British Museum. Subject Index of the Modern Works Added to the
        Library
Buyer's Guide to Microsoftware

Campus Wide Information Systems. Listserve Archive
CD-ROM Information Products
CD-ROM Market Place
CD-ROMs in Print
CERT
CERT Security Advisories
Chicago Manual of Style
Children's Books in Print
Children's Catalog
Communications of the ACM
Complete Directory of Large Print Books and Serials
Comp-priv Mailing List Archive
Comprehensive Dissertation Index
Compression and Archival Software Summary
Computer ASAP
Computer Database
Computer Ethics
The Computer Glossary
Computer News Fulltext
Computer Professional's Dictionary
Computer-readable Databases
Computer Science Archive Sites
Computer Science Paper Bibliography
Computer Science Tech Reports
Conference Papers Index
Conversational Hypertext
Corporate Technology Directory
Corporations for Research and Educational Networking
Cumulative Book Index
Current Cites
Current Technology Index
Data Sources
Dial-In
DIALINDEX
DIALOG Bluesheets
DIALOG Chronolog Newsletter
DIALOG Homebase
DIALOG Journal Name Finder
DIALOG Product Name Finder
DIALOG Publications
Dictionary Catalog of the Arthur Schomburg Collection of Negro
        Literature and History

Dictionary Catalog of the Jesse Moorland Collection of Negro Life and
    History
Dictionary Catalog of the Negro Collection of the Fisk University
    Library
Dictionary of Anonymous and Pseudonymous English Literature
Dictionary of Information Science and Technology
Dictionary of Literary Pseudonyms
Directory of Computer Conferencing in Libraries
Directory of Electronic Journals & Newsletters
Directory of Library and Information Professionals
Directory of Online Databases
Directory of Portable Databases
Directory of Special Libraries
Directory of WAIS Services
Dissertation Abstracts International
Dissertation Abstracts Ondisc
Domain Names & Organizations
Electronic Frontier Foundation
El-Hi Textbooks in Print
Elsevier's Dictionary of Library Science, Information and
    Documentation
Encyclopedia of Library and Information Science
Fiction Catalog
Fidonet Node List
Forthcoming Books
Free Software Foundation
The Gardner's Assistant
Government Printing Office Style Manual
Great Beginnings
Guide to Microforms in Print
Handbook of Organization and Membership Directory
Handbook of Pseudonyms and Personal Nicknames
Hytelnet
IETF Documents
IETF Drafts
Inet Services
Information Science Abstracts
Information System for Advanced Academic Computing
International Books in Print
International Directory of Acronyms in Library, Information and
    Computer Science
International Guide to Library, Archival, and Information Science
    Associations

Non-linear Dynamics Archive
NorthWestNet User Services. Internet Resource Guide
NRIA Bibliography
NUC AV Indexes and Register
NUC Books
Online/CD-ROM Database News
Online Resources Mailing List
Only the Best
Optical Publishing Directory
O'Reilly and Associates, Inc.
Oxford Thesaurus
PACS-L Listserv Archives
Paperbound Books in Print
PC Magazine
Prototype WAIS Ftp Server
Pseudonyms and Nickname
PSI White Pages Pilot Project
Public Library Catalog
Public UNIX Access
Publishers, Distributors, and Wholesalers
Publisher's Practical Dictionary
Publishers' Trade List Annual
Pugh's Dictionary of Acronyms and Abbreviations
Que's Computer User's Dictionary
The Reader's Advisor
REMARC
Repository of Machine Learning Databases and Domain Theories
RFC
RLIN
Senior High School Library Catalog
SGML
SIGHyper
Simulated Conversations
The Software Catalog
Subject Collections
Subject Guide to Books in Print
Subject Guide to Children's Books in Print
Subject Index of the Modern Works Added to the Library
Supernet
Supplements: Bibliographic Guide to Black Studies
U.S. Copyrights
UNIX Manual
UNIX Reference Card

UNT's Accessing On-Line Bibliographic Databases
Usenet Address
Usenet Frequently Asked Questions
Usenet Periodic Posting Archives
Usenet Software
UUNET FTP Archives
Vertical File Index
Vocabularium Bibliothecarii
WAIS Software Search Sources
What is USENET?
The Whole Internet
Who's Who in Library and Information Science
A World Bibliography of Bibliographies
World Guide to Libraries
Zen and the Art of the Internet
Zip Code Guide

CHAPTER 6

DICTIONARIES

Reference Interviews

Patron #1.   A junior high school girl.

Patron: Do you have any books on how to write papers?
Librarian: Did you want something on how to write the paper or
                 how to type it for handing in?
Patron: No, something on words in papers.
Librarian: Do you mean synonyms for words?
Patron: I guess so. What I want is to find some other words that
                 mean the same thing as my words but sound better.

                 Where would you go?

Patron #2.   A man.

Patron: I hate to bother you, but I'm helping my daughter do
                 her homework and I need help. Have you ever heard of
                 acronyms?
Librarian: Yes, I have.
Patron: Well, this dumb teacher has assigned these kids to find
                 out what AFRA and ASHA mean and I've looked and
                 can't find it. We have a big unabridged dictionary and
                 it's not even in there. Do you think that you could
                 possibly find it?

                 Where could you find the answers?

Patron #3.   A little boy.

Patron: Is decomposer the same as decompose?

Librarian:	Are you trying to decide how to use it?
Patron:	I guess.
Librarian:	Is this for a class?
Patron:	It's for science.

Where would you look?

Reference Questions

1. What is the difference between amoral, immoral, and unmoral?

2. What does Calapooya mean?

3. What does the term "cold water" mean? Why was President Hayes's administration called the "cold water regime"?

4. Jimmy Durante: "What I don't dig over there is the British money." Is the use of "dig" slang?

5. Distinguish among fearful, awful, dreadful, and frightful.

6. What is a "flyblister"?

7. When did fractional currency appear?

8. What is the meaning of "dittay"? Give several alternative spellings of the word.

9. What is the plural of "gallows": When was it first used to mean "suspenders"?

10. What is the meaning of "ha-ha" in the following quotation? "The ha! ha! is digging."

11. What is the pronunciation of Hawarden?

12. Find four antonyms for indifference.

13. What are the differences among infer, deduce, and conclude?

14. "J'y suis, j'y reste." Who said it and how is it pronounced?

15. Is "lingulate" derived from a Latin word?

16. What does "malo mori quam foedari" stand for?

17. What is a moot hall? When was the term first used? What is a mazer? A peel tower?

18. What is a musaraigne?

19. When was the term "oak openings" first used?

20. What is the distinction between noticeable and remarkable?

21. Was the word "outwit" in use before 1800?

22. Is the term "over and above" a cliché?

23. What is a packetarian?

24. What is the size of a paca?

25. AP, May 10, 1951 reported: "The jockey is in the panic rack and ready to go." What is a panic rack?

26. What is a Rahdaree?

27. What is razzamatazz?

28. What is the difference between reoccurrence and recurrence?

29. What is a rob-pot?

30. What is the meaning of "rocked in the stone kitchen"?

31. What was the Treaty of San Stefano?

32. What is a sangar?

33. Who first used sequoia as a name for a genus of trees?

34.   Was the word "soused" in use in seventeenth-century England?

35.   What is the name of the male swan? the female swan?

36.   What is the meaning of "tire" in the following quotation:
        Well-drilled urchins, each behind his tire
        Waited in ranks the wished command to fire.

37.   Was the word "tittle-tattle" in use in England in the seventeenth-century ?

38.   Who coined the word "tularemia"?

39.   What is the English meaning of the French word "arbre"?

40.   What is a "giggle-mug"?

41.   What is the distinction between the words "honorable" and "honorary"?

42.   What is the difference between "mantle" and "mantel"?

43.   How did the word "nepotism" originate?

44.   What does the term "nolo contendere" mean?

45.   What is the meaning of the expression "on the lam"?

46.   What was the origin of the expression "border ruffian"?

47.   I want the German word for "salt" with its correct use in several idioms.

48.   What is the proper form of address for use with a U.S. senator?

49.   What is the Spanish word for "shamrock"?

50.   I need a definition of the word "stethoscope," with a small picture of one.

51.   Find a list of synonyms for the word "strict."

52.   What is a Saratoga trunk?

53.   What are several nouns that might be used instead of the word "vulgarity"?

54.   Find an illustration of egg-and-dart molding.

55.   Please find the etymology of the word "mutton," with quotations illustrating its usage since 1290 A.D.

56.   I would like the definition of the French word "fier," with some literary quotations showing its usage.

57.   What does the phrase "Queen Anne is dead" imply?

58.   Find an etymology in German of the word "wissenschaftlich."

59.   Is Mexico spelled the same way in English as in Spanish?

60.   Is an armed truck transferring money from a place of business to a bank called an "armored cow"?

61.   What is nystatin?

62.   What words are derived from "cameloter"?

63.   What are some German synonyms for "interior"?

64.   What is the International Civil Aircraft Marking for Switzerland?

65.   What is the proper way to address a duke's daughter?

66.   What is the meaning of "Anschluss"?

67.   What is the origin of the word "check" in reference to checks and balances?

68.   Were the terms "ale" and "beer" originally used synonymously?

69.   Is Pago Pago pronounced pay-GO pay-GO?

70.   What is the difference between the American and British usage of the words "vacation" and "holiday"?

71.   What is the meaning of the expression, "Water under the bridge"?

72.   What are several synonymous phrases for "To give a Roland for an Oliver"?

73.   What is the meaning of "au gratin"?

74.   How long is the Mississippi River?

75.   What does the acronym ALCOA stand for?

76.   Where can I find the name of the person who said, "Rome est dans notre camp et notre camp dans Rome"?

77.   How did the meaning of the German word "armut" change over the years?

78.   Where would you look in order to find the origin of the word "anatocism"?

79.   What is an antonym for "crawl"?

80.   Find a listing of philosophers.

81.   What is the meaning of the word "groovy"?

82.   What were the main forms of "to have" in Old English?

83.   Find the source of an 1889 quotation showing Rider Haggard's use of the word "scrawl."

84.   What is an antonym for the word "feeling"?

85.   Find a photograph illustrating the definition of the word "robin."

86.   What is the FHA?

87. What is the French word for "war"?

88. Locate line drawings to illustrate the term "fever-few plant."

89. What is sunshine cake and where can you find a recipe for it?

90. What does a lyre look like?

91. What does "to make the scene" mean?

92. What were the origins of the term "apple-fritter"?

93. What is the earliest written record of the use of the American word "chaparral"?

94. Do "dobie" and "adobe" have different meanings?

95. Find a list of expressions which include the word "boot," and when they originated in the U.S.

96. Locate a picture of a lowboy.

97. What is the meaning of the term "sugar daddy"?

98. What does the expression "bring home the bacon" mean?

99. What is the meaning of "ogfray"?

100. What are the differences in the meanings of the terms "intend" and "mean"?

101. Find an antonym for the word "meager."

102. What is the difference in meaning between "connote" and "denote"?

103. Find a list of synonyms for the word "happy."

104. What does the expression "armored cow" mean?

105. What were the origins of the expression "cracker barrel"?

106.   Locate antonyms and analogous words for the word "surprised."

107.   Is "fiord" or fjord" the correct English spelling?

108.   Find a discussion and examples of the uses and abuses of inversion in writing.

109.   What is the meaning of the expression, "to shed light upon the subject"?

110.   What is the difference between the British and the American usage of the word "trunk"?

111.   Compare the meanings of the words "rare" and "scarce."

112.   What is the Roman numeral for 3,000?

113.   What is the military time equivalent for 12:15 A.M.?

114.   What does MOBOT stand for?

115.   What is the initialism for "general intelligence"?

116.   What is the FLW?

117.   What does UNICEF stand for?

118.   Locate a list of synonyms for the word "necessary."

119.   What were the major world events of the 1450s?

120.   What does "logo" mean?

121.   Find synonyms and antonyms for the word "sweet."

122.   What is a "moonshiner"?

123.   Find an etymology of the word "shoe," with quotations showing its usage since 1150 A.D.

124.   What does ROCMM stand for?

125.   What does "modus vivendi" mean?

126.   Do "machine screw" and "machine steel" have the same initialism?

127.   Find a definition of the word "naskin," which was used in Great Britain in about 1670-1830.

128.   Was the phrase, "to lie in wait," used in the English language before 1620?

129.   What is the meaning of the phrase, "si fortuna juvat"?

130.   Find the German equivalents of "down and out" and "down - Easter."

131.   What is the Spanish equivalent of the verb "help"?

132.   Locate the etymology of the word "Geschichte."

133.   What is the etymology of the Spanish term "infanteria"?

134.   What does an Englishman mean when he speaks of his "hat covering his family"?

135.   Where can one find translations of the words referring to the parts of a camera?

136.   What do the abbreviations, "ss fx," "bldi," and "4R" stand for?

137.   Find a lengthy discussion with quotations on the meanings of the Spanish word "abreviar."

138.   What is a "ding-a-ling"?

139.   Find a historical summary of the meanings and uses of the German word "erarbeiten."

140. What is the acronym for the solar energy research firm, Energy Conversion Devices?

141. What is a "flutter wheel"? When and by whom was it patented?

142. What is the German word for "carfare"?

143. What is a "daftar"?

144. What does NATO stand for?

145. What is the Beecher's Bible?

146. What time of year is Adar?

147. How is the word "mesdames" pronounced?

148. How is the word "pekinese" spelled?

149. What is the Latin name for the swamp privet?

150. What is a "hillbilly"?

151. How long is a fathom?

152. Where was Ferdinand, King of Aragon, born?

153. What is a dandelion?

154. What is the current use of the word "consensus"?

155. What is the meaning of the term "hematogenesis"?

156. What does the word "polar" mean?

157. Where is Shasta?

158. What does the word "nudnick" mean?

159. What is Oxygen Point?

160.   A Civil War novel I'm reading keeps talking about greenbacks; what are they anyways?

161.   My grandmother said that as a child she made "bone lace." Where can I find a definition of this term?

162.   What is the origin of the word "house"?

163.   When would one use the word "paranoiac" versus the word "paranoid"?

164.   Where could I find an explanation of the expression "top dog"?

165.   What is the French word for "lipstick"?

166.   Where can I find proof that "it's" can be used as a pronoun? I want to show it to my English teacher.

167.   Where and when did the term "airline" originate?

168.   What is a serac?

169.   What is the German word for librarian?

170.   What does the word "amuck" mean? Is it related to "amok"?

171.   What does "bibliotecario" mean?

172.   Where can I find a definition and pronunciation for the German word "Festschrift"?

173.   I was reading an article on academic freedom and it mentioned the German concepts of *Lehrfrieheit* and *Lernfreiheit* — can you help me find out what these are?

174.   I'm reading a book on German literature and keep running into this phrase *Sturm und Drang*. What does it mean?

175.   Where can I find an illustration of cat's cradle?

176. I am writing an essay in French, and I don't like the sound of a word I've chosen. How can I find a better word? I'm very uncomfortable with my French.

177. My friend thinks the term "lady" shows respect, I think it is more of an insult. Who is correct?

178. Where would I find synonyms for the word "sympathetic"?

179. Where did the term "caucus" originate? What is its earliest recorded use?

180. What is "bundling"?

181. Which is more appropriate to say in an art history paper, that the statue was "naked" or "nude"?

182. In what region did the word "batea" first enter the English language, and what does it mean?

183. I heard a bully at school call someone a bunch of names that I didn't understand and couldn't find in the regular dictionary — is there somewhere that I can look these up?

184. I was reading this mystery novel and there was a reference to NEMQO. Can you tell me what it means?

185. Find a picture of a derrick.

186. What is the origin of the word "Bible"?

187. Which of these is correct — "He had awoken" or "He had awaked"?

188. What is the origin of the word "sailor"?

189. Where can I find the meaning behind the saying "out of the frying pan" followed by a brief essay describing it?

190. Where can I quickly find the Braille alphabet?

191.   What is a "baiser de paix"?

192.   While reading *The Once and Future King* by T.H. White, I came across "fewmets" and would like to know the origin of the word.

193.   How many definitions of the word "bright" are there?

194.   When was the word "brigand" first used as a term for robber?

195.   What does "furp" mean?

196.   How is the word "zaglossus" pronounced?

197.   What is the proper way to use the word "which" in sentences?

198.   My paper was downgraded because of a "mixed metaphor." What does the teacher mean?

Reference Materials

Abbreviations Dictionary
Acronyms, Initialisms and Abbreviations Dictionary
The American College Dictionary
American Heritage Dictionary of the English Language
Appleton's New Cuyás English-Spanish and Spanish-English
        Dictionary
Bernstein's Reverse Dictionary
Cassell's French Dictionary
Cassell's German Dictionary
Cassell's Spanish Dictionary
Children's World Book Dictionary
Deutsches Wörterbuch
Diccionario de la lengua española
Dictionnaire alphabétique et analogique de la langue française
A Dictionary of American English on Historical Principles
Dictionary of American Slang
A Dictionary of Americanisms

A Dictionary of Contemporary American Usage
Dictionary of Foreign Phrases and Abbreviations
Dictionary of Foreign Terms
Dictionary of Modern English Usage
A Dictionary of Slang and Unconventional English
Fund and Wagnalls New Standard Dictionary of the English Language
Funk and Wagnalls Standard College Dictionary
Harper Dictionary of Contemporary Usage
Harrap's New Standard French and English Dictionary
Kister's Best Dictionaries for Adults and Young People
Der Kleine Muret Sanders
Langenscheidt's New Muret-Sanders Encyclopedic Dictionary of
          English and German Languages
Larousse Modern French-English (English-French) Dictionary
NBC Handbook of Pronunciations
Oxford Dictionary of New Words
Oxford English Dictionary
Random House Dictionary of the English Language
Random House Webster's College Dictionary
Reverse Acronyms, Initialisms and Abbreviations Dictionary
Roget's Thesaurus
Scott, Foresman Beginning Dictionary
Scott, Foresman Intermediate Dictionary
Thorndike-Barnhart Advanced Junior Dictionary
Webster's Collegiate Thesaurus
Webster's Dictionary of English Usage
Webster's New Collegiate Dictionary
Webster's New World Dictionary
Webster's Third New International Dictionary of the English Language
World Book Dictionary

CHAPTER 7

HANDBOOKS

Reference Interviews

Patron #1.   A woman.

Patron: I'm giving a Christmas party, and I want to know how
               to do it.
Librarian: Do you mean that you want party plans, food recipes,
               plans for decorating—things like that?
Patron: No, more what I should do: what's proper.
Librarian: Do you mean how to be a hostess?
Patron: Yes.

               Where would you find this information?

Patron #2.   A middle-aged woman.

Patron: I'd like some information about eating.
Librarian: What sort of information?
Patron: Well, my daughter and I had an argument about
               asparagus. She said that you should eat it with your
               fingers and I said that was sloppy. So, I thought that
               you might have some sort of book that would tell me
               who was right.

               Where would you look?

Patron #3.   An elderly woman.

Patron: Do you have any books about clubs?

Librarian:	Yes, we do. What sort of book did you have in mind? How to form a club, parliamentary procedure, fund raising ideas, etc.?
Patron:	I don't exactly know. I've just been elected president of my church group, and I don't know all those rules about bringing meetings to order, passing motions, and things like that.

What would you suggest?

Patron #4. A high school girl.

Patron:	Can you help me? We had a discussion in history class today and I've been assigned to find out the answer.
Librarian:	What was the discussion about?
Patron:	It was about the first American child. My teacher said it was Virginia Dare, but some kids in my class disagreed.
Librarian:	What do you mean by American? Do you mean the first child born in North America of European parents or the first child born in an English colony, or what?
Patron:	I guess the first child born in America of parents from any European country.

Where could you find the answer?

Patron #5 An elementary school teacher.

Patron:	Do you have any books about Halloween?
Librarian:	Do you want a collection of spooky stories and, if so, for what reading level?
Patron:	I don't want story books. I'm teaching a sixth grade class this year, and I want to tell them the history of Halloween and how it's celebrated in other countries.

Where would you look?

Patron #6. A man.

Patron: I heard something on the radio a few weeks ago about
               the largest check ever written on a bank. I think it was
               paid to Sears, but I'm not sure. It may have been
               Montgomery Ward or J.C. Penney. Anyway, could you
               find out some more information about it for me?
Librarian: How much information do you need?
Patron: Oh, I'd like to know how much it was for and what
               bank it was written on and who it was paid to.

               Where is the answer?

Patron #7.   A high school boy.

Patron: Do you have any dictionaries of history?
Librarian: What was it you wanted to know—the meaning of some
               term?
Patron: Not exactly. I don't want to bother reading a whole
               long encyclopedia article or book on something. I just
               want to find a short synopsis.
Librarian: Is this a historical period or event or person?
Patron: The New Deal.

               Where could you find a brief synopsis?

Reference Questions

1. What is the origin of April Fool's Day?

2. Who is the tallest woman in the world?

3. Has any person ever lifted more than a ton?

4. What university offered the first bibliography course? When?

5. To what did "corduroy roads" refer in the period of American
    westward expansion?

6. How did Candlemas Day get its name?

7.   What is the proper size for a business card?

8.   Is it possible to amend a resolution of censure by replacing the word "censure" with "thanks"?

9.   Which baseball outfielder was called "Cherokee" and why?

10. What is "chronom-hoton-theolgos"?

11. When was the football dummy introduced to aid in teaching tackling?

12. What was the *Ecbasis Captivi*?

13. Who made the first fire engine built in this country?

14. Which first lady was known as the "Bonny Brown Wife"?

15. Who was the "fraud President"?

16. What city is known as the Gibraltar of Louisiana?

17. Who was "the girl with the ginger-snap name"?

18. What is the opening line of a story in verse, published in the 19th century, about a goose which the cook sent to the table with only one leg?

19. What is Hognor Bread?

20. Who invented the ice-making machine of the vapor compression type?

21. Which firm of architects designed Iowa's state capitol building?

22. Which state is known as the Italy of America?

23. Who would use a "jesse" and what is it?

24. What are the names of the three Graces?

25. Who was Kiddo?

26. What did the Know Ye Party advocate?

27. What was significant about the establishment of the Contra
     Costa Laundry in the U.S. in 1851?

28. When were American soldiers first granted free mailing
     privileges?

29. What day belonged to the Lord of Misrule?

30. What was the Mississippi Bubble?

31. Who wrote the words to Joseph R. Howard's *Montana* ?

32. Who originated the idea of Mother's Day?

33. The motto of which American state is in Spanish?

34. What state is known as the Mud-Cat state?

35. What American President had a Newspaper Cabinet?

36. How long does it take to boil an ostrich egg?

37. When is Patriots' Day celebrated?

38. Pelota was introduced to early 16th-century Spain by Hernando
     Cortez as a "merry festival"; what is its American name or
     equivalent?

39. In which world war did "Red One" fight?

40. What is the remotest island in the world and what are the two
     nearest land masses?

41. Stalky, McTurk and Beetle were all based on real people; who
     are they?

42. How much should one tip?

43. What did the Wisconsin capitol cost?

44. Where was the first watch repair shop in the U.S. located?

45. How did Indiana get its nickname?

46. Where is the world's largest flag?

47. What was the year in which the first Thanksgiving Day was celebrated in America?

48. What was the name of the first university building in America?

49. To which famous couple do the English consecrate May Day?

50. Where can you find information which would help a student of literature identify "Grishkin" and the "Brazilian Jaguar" in T.S. Eliot's "Whispers of Immortality"?

51. When was football first played in the U.S.?

52. By what name was Mary Todd called before her marriage to Abe Lincoln?

53. What is the correct table setting for the bridal party?

54. When was the first rebellion of colonists against the English?

55. What "firsts" have occurred on April 28 in the U.S.?

56. What colors are permissible for a debutante's dress?

57. The world's largest overdue book fine was recorded a number of years ago. For how much was it, and how long had the book been due?

58. What appellations have been given James Knox Polk?

59. What does the word "pole" mean?

60. Why is "Eureka" the motto of California?

61.   When was the first American fire engine made?

62.   Who was the heaviest man ever to be weighed officially?

63.   What city was given the name "Flower City"?

64.   Who was the "Harness Horse of the Year" in 1947 (as selected by Nation's Turf Writers)?

65.   What are the correct procedures for a military wedding?

66.   Where could I find a bibliography of books about American patriotic holidays?

67.   Which U.S. president coined the term "muckracker" and to what character does it refer?

68.   Should the word "mister" be written in full or abbreviated on a wedding invitation?

69.   Where is the world's largest castle located?

70.   What is the world's gastronomic record for eating bananas?

71.   Who holds the record for non-stop talking?

72.   Find a brief biography of Eleanor of Aquitaine, Queen of Louis VII.

73.   Locate a summary of *The Odyssey*.

74.   Find an explanation of existentialism.

75.   Identify Anna Karenina.

76.   What are some of the "firsts" for Ann Arbor, Michigan?

77.   What events happened on December 19, 1620?

78.   Locate a bibliography of materials for information about the red legs of the Civil War.

79.   What was "Seward's Folly"?

80.   Who was the Borax King?

81.   Which college athletes are known as the Lord Jeffs?

82.   How does one write a bread-and-butter note?

83.   What is the proper attire for a formal evening wedding?

84.   What is the proper method of recessing a meeting?

85.   How does one second a motion?

86.   What is the correct form for the minutes of a meeting?

87.   What are the duties of a treasurer of an organization?

88.   What are the positions and numbers for a game of volleyball?

89.   Locate information about the history of archery.

90.   How does one run a round robin tournament?

91.   What is the proper manner for making an introduction at a party?

92.   Find a summary of *King Lear* .

93.   Locate a list of National League batting champions since 1901.

94.   Must you be recognized by the chair before seconding a motion?

95.   Where is the world's longest suspension bridge?

96.   Who made the first non-stop, cross-country airplane flight in the U.S.?

97.   How did the nickname "Hoosier" originate for the state of Indiana?

98. How does one set the table for a small buffet?

99. What are the rules for scoring a bowling game?

100. Who was the first astronaut in the U.S.?

101. What is the correct way to announce the arrival of a new baby?

102. Find a history of golf.

103. Identify the literary character Raskolnikov.

104. What are the duties of a vice-president of an organization?

105. Who is the world's fattest man?

106. Who was the "Poet of the American Revolution"?

107. How does one use finger-bowls when dining?

108. How does one fill out a baseball box card?

109. Find a summary of the novel *Alice Adams* by Booth Tarkington.

110. How did Idaho get its name?

111. Who was the first baseball pitcher to pitch a perfect no-hit, no-run, no-walk World Series game?

112. What is the tallest man-made structure in the world?

113. What is the "realistic" school of literature?

114. Did Albert Camus ever read R.L. Stevenson's *Weir of Hermiston*?

115. What is the proper form for addressing the pope in conversation?

116. Should the treasurer's report be included in the secretary's minutes?

117.   Should one say, "Lydia, this is Paul," or "Paul, this is Lydia"?

118.   Who was "Old Gimlet Eye"?

119.   Find a synopsis of *Paradise Lost*.

120.   In what novel is Bill Sikes a character?

121.   Should an invitation to a wedding reception be acknowledged?

122.   Who first used anesthesia?

123.   Into what three states does Yellowstone National Park extend?

124.   What goes in the constitution and by-laws of a club?

125.   Where do the speaker and the president sit at a speakers' table?

126.   Can a negative vote concerning a parliamentary inquiry be reconsidered?

127.   Who pays for various wedding expenses?

128.   Where may one find advice on letters of condolence?

129.   What store had the first escalator in the U.S.?

130.   When a registered delegate of a convention wishes to end his or her presence, to what body must the departure be reported?

131.   Find a synopsis of *The Three Musketeers*.

132.   What is an appropriate gift for a fifteenth wedding anniversary?

133.   What was the first school for higher education for women in the U.S.?

134.   When was the first time Franklin Delano Roosevelt appeared on television?

135.   Who was Dulcinea del Toboso?

136.   William Faulkner keeps referring to Yoknapatawpha County in his novels, is this a real place?

137.   I'd like to read a brief background of the development of French-Canadian literature. Where would I look?

138.   Where can I find a description of post-modern fiction?

139.   When did the first automobile accident occur?

140.   Where could I find a brief synopsis of Milton's *Paradise Lost*?

141.   When and where did the world's strongest earthquake happen?

142.   When I eat cherries, is it rude if I remove the pits with my hands?

143.   Why is the Goose Bible called thus?

144.   What was Millard Fillmore's nickname as president?

145.   When was the first Librarians' Convention?

146.   Who is currently the most prolific author in the world?

147.   When were football referees first allowed to use television instant replay in making calls?

148.   Who (or what institution) developed the first bibliography course?

149.   What is the depth record for diving without the assistance of an underwater breathing apparatus?

150.   My sister says Beethoven wrote the longest symphony, but I think it was Mahler. Where can I find out which of us is correct?

151.   What were the events surrounding the beginning of the traditional Thanksgiving celebration?

152.   What is the most dangerous animal in the world?

153.   I want to serve artichokes at my next party but I am not sure
        how you eat them. Can you help?

154.   What is the name of the first daily newspaper to be published in
        the U.S.?

155.   How much does one tip a hotel bell-boy? Is it polite to tip
        airline attendants?

156.   I need a description of *The Nibelungenleid* that Wagner used for
        his opera.

157.   Who wrote stories about Troilus and Cressida, and in which
        literary forms were they written?

158.   Where did soda water originate?

159.   My cousin made a map that I think must have broken a world
        record. Can you tell me how big the largest map in the world
        is?

160.   Which state was the first to have a town with a woman mayor?
        When was she elected and what was her name and her age
        when elected? Also, how long did she serve and how much did
        she get paid?

161.   Was the nomadic lifestyle portrayed in Paul Bowles's novel *The
        Sheltering Sky* autobiographical in nature?

162.   What is the significance of the Thanksgiving holiday?

163.   What is *The Last of the Mohicans* about?

164.   Who wrote the poem "America the Beautiful," and when?

165.   When was basketball invented and who invented it?

166.   Who was the shortest U.S. president?

167.   Our school is having a jump rope contest fund raiser, and we were wondering what the highest number of jumps in a row was?

168.   When was the pinball game invented?

169.   Where can I find out about a character in some book called Man Friday?

170.   Is it proper to give a shower for someone expecting their second child?

171.   Where can I find the genealogy of William Faulkner's character Bayard Sartois?

172.   What is the proper way to set the table for a formal dinner?

173.   I want to give a party on January 23. Is there a special anniversary or event for that day that I can use as a theme?

Reference Materials

All About American Holidays
American Book of Days
American Nicknames
The Amy Vanderbilt Complete Book of Etiquette
Anniversaries and Holidays
Benet's Reader's Encyclopedia
Chases' Calendar of Annual Events
Dictionary of Phrase & Fable
The Dictionary of Sports
The Encyclopedia of Sports
Facts About the Presidents
Famous First Facts
Festivals Sourcebook
Guinness Book of World Records
Miss Manners' Guide
The New Emily Post's Etiquette

Notes and Queries
Number One in the U.S.A.
The Reader's Encyclopedia
Recipes
Robert's Rules of Order Newly Revised
Scarne's Encyclopedia of Games
State Names, Flags, Seals, Songs, Birds, Flowers and Other Symbols
Wedding Planner

CHAPTER 8

SERIAL PUBLICATIONS

Reference Interviews

Patron #1.   A young boy.

Patron: Where can I find ... I'm doing a report on fishing, ship
              building, livestock, and ships. I think that's all.
Librarian: That's a lot. Do you mean livestock like farm animals
              or are you talking about stocking water with fish?
Patron: Farm animals.
Librarian: Do you want books to take home?
Patron: If you have any. All my material is supposed to be
              about recent developments in the last year.

              Where would you look first?

Patron #2.   A high school girl.

Patron: Where do you keep the books on black problems. I
              can't find anything in the card catalog.
Librarian: Is it recent black problems that you have in mind?
Patron: Yes. It's for current events class.
Librarian: Your best source for current events is magazines and
              newspapers.
Patron: I have to know, too, how people reacted to the death of
              Martin Luther King.

              Where could you find this information?

Patron #3.   An older man.

Patron: I'm investigating the Pueblo Incident. I want to know
                what happened then. You know, what the status of the
                whole affair is at present.
Librarian: The Pueblo Incident was in January of 1968, wasn't it?
Patron: Yes, that's right.

                Where would you look?

Patron #4.   A high school girl.

Patron: I need some book reviews on Muhammed.
Librarian: Is that the name of a book?
Patron: Yes.
Librarian: Do you know who the author is or when it was
                published?
Patron: No.
Librarian: Do you have the book with you?
Patron: Yes.
Librarian: We need to know the name of the author. Here she is.
                It's by Ruth Warren and this gives the year of
                publication.
Patron: So where do I go now for reviews?

                Where could you find reviews?

Patron #5.   A man.

Patron: I want to find out what has happened to Powell
                recently.
Librarian: Do you mean Adam Clayton Powell?
Patron: The former congressman.
Librarian: How recently do you mean—in the last week or month?
Patron: I need to know since the Supreme Court ruled the
                House of Representatives action unconstitutional.
Librarian: Do you know what date that was?
Patron: No.

                Where would you check?

Patron #6.   A local general practitioner.

Patron:	I need some information on abortions.
Librarian:	Have you checked the card catalog and pamphlet file?
Patron:	Yes. You don't have what I want.
Librarian:	Did you want something more recent?
Patron:	Yes. I want to find out some of the international viewpoints on abortion.

Where would you look?

Patron #7. A woman.

Patron:	Has Anne Sexton died?
Librarian:	The poet?
Patron:	Yes, the American poet.
Librarian:	If she had died, it would have been recently?
Patron:	Yes.

Where could you check?

Patron #8. A high school boy.

| Patron: | I'm doing the pro side of a debate on the grape boycott for my high school English class. Where can I get some information? |

Where could you check?

Patron #9. A high school girl.

Patron:	Do you have any information on Thor Heyerdahl, who wrote *Kon Tiki*?
Librarian:	There aren't any books on him as a writer.
Patron:	What I want are reviews of his writing.

Where could you find reviews?

Patron #10. A woman.

| Patron: | I'm looking for a book on publishing. |

Librarian:	What aspect of publishing did you have in mind?
Patron:	Oh, the names of different editors.
Librarian:	In the book industry?
Patron:	No, for magazines.
Librarian:	Did you have one magazine in mind?
Patron:	Yes, I wanted to know the editor of the magazine *Human Events*.

Where could you find this information?

Patron #11. A girl.

Patron:	Does the library have issues of magazines from the 1930s?
Librarian:	Yes, we do—some of the more popular magazines, such as *Time, Life,* and *Saturday Evening Post*. Are you looking for a certain topic?
Patron:	Yes—discrimination against the American Indians in the 1930s, and what was happening to them at that time.

Where would you look?

Patron #12. A high school boy.

Patron:	Do you have information on the Suez Canal?
Librarian:	What type of information?
Patron:	I want to find out what happened in the conflict there. Not what happened in the area of the canal but only the events that occurred right on the canal itself—the dates it opened and closed.

Where would you look for detailed information?

Patron #13. A young woman.

| Patron: | Do you have any recent articles on swapping wives? |

Where would you look?

Patron #14. A woman.

Patron:	I would like to get some information about the Bataan Death March.
Librarian:	What kind of information do you need?
Patron:	I just found out that my father-in-law was one of the prisoners, and I would like to read some magazine articles about what happened.

Where would you find periodical articles?

Reference Questions

1. How much of the series, *Masters in Art,* is owned by Allegheny College?

2. Does any American library have a complete file of the *Arkhiv* of the Institut Marksa-Engelsa-Lenina?

3. What are the names of the principal college newspapers in Illinois?

4. Who wrote an article on the "Art of Plagiarism" which appeared in a magazine in 1904?

5. Where can you find information on the early files of the newspaper *The Boston Recorder*?

6. Locate libraries in the U.S. that have files of the *China Journal.* Do any Canadian libraries have it?

7. In what magazine did George Meredith's *Diana of the Crossways* appear in the 1880s?

8. Can you find a review of *Jane Eyre* by Charlotte Brontë, by one of her contemporaries?

9. Did Zechariah Fowle have anything to do with the *Exeter* [New Hampshire] *Journal* in 1778-1779?

10.   Locate E.A. Freeman's review of Grote's *History of Greece*, written in the middle of the nineteenth century.

11.   In what libraries can the publications of the K. Freie ökonomische Gesellschaft zu St. Petersburg be found?

12.   Which serial does *Quarterly Demographic Bulletin*, which began publication in 1979, continue?

13.   Who wrote the article, "On the Trail of Geronimo," in the 1880s?

14.   What is the oldest newspaper in Lexington, Massachusetts? Is there a complete file of it?

15.   What is the circulation of the *Lincoln* [Nebraska] *Journal*?

16.   How much of the series, *Master in Music*, does the Nashville Public Library possess?

17.   What is the aggregate circulation of all morning and evening newspapers in the U.S.?

18.   Find a list of Latin American newspapers.

19.   Does the *Journal* of the American Oil Chemists Society have abstracts or book reviews?

20.   Locate current articles in American periodicals on the televising of sports.

21.   Where did George DuMaurier's *Trilby* appear in the 1890s?

22.   Who is the editor of the London *Daily Express*?

23.   I need a copy of the *Lafayette Evening Call*, a newspaper published in Lafayette, Indiana from 1883-1905. Where can I find it?

24.   What is the circulation of the Montreal newspaper *La Presse*?

25. Find a chronological index to news stories about Spanish politics and government which appeared last year.

26. Do any libraries in the U.S. have a copy of Volume Three of *Semaine des enfants,* a French serial publication?

27. Locate news articles about Walt Disney's illness and death in 1966.

28. How often does *Who's Who in the Midwest* appear?

29. Are there any magazines on camping published in California?

30. What are the names and addresses of some manufacturers and suppliers of rotary presses used by newspapers?

31. Does the Illinois State Library have complete holdings of the *Japanese Journal of Botany* from 1922 to 1949?

32. How often is the *Clinical Reporter*, a serial which began in 1962, published?

33. In what languages is the magazine *Mines* available?

34. Where is *Sports Illustrated* indexed?

35. I would like a list, with short summaries, of recent newspaper articles on NATO.

36. Find a list of periodicals on the subject of international trade.

37. Find statistics about newspaper publishing in New York state.

38. Find a list of American libraries which have copies of the annual report of the Shanghai Meteorological Society.

39. Locate a historical sketch, as well as library holdings, of the newspaper *The Massachusetts Spy*, from 1775 to 1820.

40. Who publishes *Bibliothèque*, the journal of the Ecole des Chartes? What is its price?

41.   What periodical deals with traffic management?

42.   Who is the editor of *Canadian Swine?*

43.   Jackie Robinson was admitted to major league baseball in 1945. Where can I find newspaper accounts about this event and about racial discrimination in organized baseball during that year?

44.   Where can I find an article on the canal system of Canada written in the nineteenth century?

45.   I want to find the initial reactions of reviewers to Margaret Mitchell's *Gone with the Wind*. Where can I locate some of those old reviews?

46.   Where can I find newspaper articles which appeared immediately after the death of Amelia Earhart in 1937?

47.   Where can I find an article on the career of King Edward VII of England?

48.   William Manchester's *Death of a President* received mixed reactions from the press. Where can I find the pro and con reactions by the reviewers?

49.   How can I locate a text of U Thant's address to the convocation of Pacem in Terris II?

50.   How can I find an article on French feelings toward Germany in 1891?

51.   Where can I find an article about George Keats, brother of the poet, written during his lifetime?

52.   How did the *New York Times* report the political viewpoints and activities of Representative Martin Dies, Chairman of the House Committee investigating un-American activities in the late 1930s?

53.   In conjunction with research on the development of advertising during the years from 1895 to 1910, I need to examine

newspapers from that era. I prefer to do the research in the Philadelphia area. What nearby institutions have newspaper files for this period?

54. Where can I find an article by G.T. Winston about high education in the South in 1897?

55. Where can one locate a criticism of the movie *Bus Stop* when it originally appeared?

56. I need to know the years when John Fenno printed the *Gazette of the United States*.

57. Is there a complete run of the *Spectator* in the U.S.?

58. I would like to know the subscription price to libraries and the circulation of *Chemical Abstracts*.

59. Are there any Estonian publications in Canada?

60. Where could one find articles about ophthalmology indexed?

61. What subjects does *The Topicator Index* cover?

62. Locate a periodical article about fireproof construction printed before 1881.

63. Locate a 1929 article about abolishing Sunday.

64. Where would one find a list of reviews of last year's television programs?

65. In which periodical index could one find references to articles about quadraphonic sound systems?

66. Locate a reference in a popular magazine about economic conditions in Japan.

67. Where would one find a list of periodical indexes in the field of anthropology?

68. In which periodical did an article by Henry James entitled "Daumier, the Caricaturist" appear in the late nineteenth century?

69. Locate a list of daily newspapers published in Massachusetts.

70. Find a list of serial publications about bridges.

71. Locate the name of a Chinese daily newspaper published in Vancouver, B.C.

72. Does the *New York Times* accept mail order advertising?

73. Who is the manager of the circulation department of the *Milwaukee Journal*?

74. Find a list of current periodicals concerned with native Americans.

75. Does *The Journal of Social Sciences* have book reviews?

76. What is the circulation of the *Hawaii AFL-CIO News?*

77. Where is *The British Journal of Radiology* indexed?

78. When did *The Atlantic Magazine* begin publication?

79. How much does a subscription to *Time* cost?

80. Which Canadian libraries receive *Norois,* a French geographic magazine which began publication in 1954?

81. What are the names of current periodicals published about the grocery trade?

82. When was *Whitaker's Almanack* founded?

83. Find a list of periodicals concerning the hotel industry.

84. Find a citation to a news article about funeral plans for John Steinbeck.

85.   Locate a list of magazine articles about Benjamin Disraeli published during the nineteenth century.

86.   How often is *Theoretical Chemical Engineering Abstracts,* which began publication in 1964, issued?

87.   Who publishes the serial *Rio Grande do Sul?*

88.   Who are the chief editors of the Fairfield, Iowa *Ledger,* a daily newspaper?

89.   What is the address of the publishers of the *Frozen Foods Year Book?*

90.   Who has copies of the *Los Angeles Times* for 1900?

91.   Locate periodical articles about sports on television.

92.   Locate a reference to an obituary of Virgil Grissom, the astronaut from the U.S.

93.   Which newspapers did William A. Davis print between 1802 - 1803?

84.   What is the price for a subscription to *Banker's Magazine?*

95.   Find a list of libraries which have copies of *Crawdaddy,* a musical periodical which began publication in 1966.

96.   What libraries have copies of the 1817 editions of the *Detroit Gazette?*

97.   Find references to periodical articles about the economic conditions in Europe which were published between 1870 and 1880.

98.   In which work would be found a reference to a periodical article on factory management written in the second decade of the nineteenth century?

99.   Does the University of Maine Library receive copies of the periodical, *Human Relations News of Chicago*, which came out in 1959?

100.   What magazine superseded the *Intellectual Observer*, which ceased publication in 1868?

101.   Does any library have a copy of the January 20, 1838 issue of the Chicago *American*, a newspaper?

102.   Find a list, with short summaries, of recent newspaper articles on NATO.

103.   How much does the *Year Book of Obstetrics and Gynecology* cost?

104.   What libraries have copies of the periodical, *Doctor's Wife*, published between 1960 and 1962?

105.   Which libraries have copies of a magazine called *Shipmate*, which began in 1938?

106.   Locate information on the *Pennsylvania Gazette*, a newspaper published between 1728 and 1815.

107.   What library has copies of the periodical, *Shoe and Leather Facts*, which was published from 1889 to 1938?

108.   What is the circulation for the Chicago *Tribune*?

109.   In what libraries could one find the American Association of School Librarians' *Newsletter*, which began publication in 1951?

110.   What is the address of the publisher of the Catholic Library Association's *Directory*?

111.   Who publishes the *Pottery Quarterly*?

112.   Locate periodical articles on Israel for a high school term paper.

113. Locate periodical articles on the Middle East for a club's program.

114. Find periodical articles on employment of the handicapped.

115. Locate periodical articles on ceramics.

116. Locate periodical articles on the family.

117. Find periodical articles on conditions in France.

118. Locate periodical articles on problems of young people.

119. Locate periodical articles about the conditions of Navaho Indians.

120. Find references to articles on present-day employment compared with that of the past.

121. Find periodical articles on planning a family budget.

122. Locate references to reviews of plays on Broadway.

123. Find periodical articles on the Depression of the 1930s.

124. Find periodical articles on women in industry.

125. Find periodical articles on the political situation in Italy.

126. Find periodical articles on the accomplishments of the United Nations during the past year.

127. What are some of the pros and cons of euthanasia?

128. Find a list of periodical articles on cybernetics.

129. Find a list of recent periodical articles on heart disease.

130. Find periodical articles on socialized medicine.

131. Find book reviews of *The Big Fisherman*.

132.   Locate periodical articles about UNESCO.

133.   Find periodical articles on spastic children.

134.   Locate periodical articles for a high school paper on genocide.

135.   Locate periodical articles for a paper on communism.

136.   Locate periodical articles about the effects of nicotine on the heart.

137.   Find magazine articles on the status of women in the USSR.

138.   Find periodical articles on recent labor legislation.

139.   Locate reviews of O'Hara's *Rage to Live*.

140.   Find materials for a paper on "Alaska Today."

141.   Locate materials for a speech on Americanism.

142.   Locate materials on some of the latest progress in the field of medicine.

143.   Find materials for a paper on the countries of southwest Asia.

144.   Find a list of periodical articles on how to reduce fat on the hips and the waist.

145.   What are the addresses of some ophthalmic publications?

146.   What is the leading newspaper in Sioux City, Iowa?

147.   Find reviews of *The Cocktail Party* by T.S. Eliot.

148.   Find a review of *Maria Theresa* by Bright, published in 1897.

149.   What are some of the titles published in the monograph series of the *Community Mental Health Journal*?

150.   Where is the magazine *Hardware Retailer* published?

151. What is the abbreviation for the *American Journal of Nursing* ?

152. What is the address of the Argus Publishers Corporation?

153. Locate a list of periodical articles about collegiate basketball.

154. Find references to recent newspaper articles about protests by university students in France.

155. My kids want me to buy some game software for our computer. I'd like to find a review about it, but don't want anything that's too technical.

156. There is a magazine called *Astro Signs* I would like to subscribe to. Can you help me find the address?

157. Where is *Scientific American* indexed?

158. What indexes index the journal, *Conservation Biology*?

159. Where could I find the address of the *East African Geographical Review?*

160. What is the subscription information for the magazine *Japanese Science and Technology / Nihon No Kagaku to Gijutsu*?

161. Where can I find color photos and detailed information of the Cincinnati Reds during their 1989 season?

162. Who publishes the journal *Scarcity*?

163. What is the inflight magazine of Delta Airlines and when was it established?

164. I want to find four-star restaurants in Italy. I know *Gourmet* writes about the topic; could you tell me where it is indexed?

165. How could one find out about all available "how-to-do-it" information?

166.   Where could review abstracts of Leonard B. Myer's book, *Style and Music: Theory, History and Ideology*?

167.   Is the Seattle *Weekly* indexed and, if so, where?

168.   My daughter is in high school and she has to do a paper on some environmental topic. She wants to write on that big oil spill in Alaska that was in the news a few years ago and the teacher says she has to use 5 magazine articles – where do we start?

169.   Where can I find a review on the video, "Single Mothers: Living on the Edge," to see whether or not I want to show it to my study group?

170.   Anthony Morgan is a modern dancer of the Graham School. He was a visiting artist at my college, and I would like to know more about his work and reactions to his choreography.

171.   I will be driving to California in a car with no cassette player. Can you give me the call numbers of some classic rock radio stations along the way?

172.   What do I use to find magazine articles about Diana, Princess of Wales?

173.   Is *Business Week* available online? From which vendor?

174.   I'm biking Europe next year; which biking magazines have articles on mountain bike travel?

175.   What are the author, title, and exact date of the 1991 article about opossums that appeared in *The Conservationist*?

176.   I'm writing a review of the movie *JFK* for a film class and I need to look at other reviews of this movie — where can I find a listing of such reviews?

177.   I bought the book *A Day in the Life of Wilbur Robinson* for my daughter and we really enjoyed it. I believe William Joyce has written some other things. Do you know if his other books are as good as *Wilbur Robinson*? And what age group are they for?

178. I want to set up an informational interview at WJAR-TV in Providence, RI. Where can I find some background information on this company including the phone number, who to contact, and the size of the organization?

179. Which reference source would a librarian wishing to select periodicals for an agriculture library consult?

180. I'm a stamp collector and have heard of a magazine called *Postal History U.S.A.* Can I find an address to write to for a subscription?

181. Does the University of Pennsylvania subscribe to *The Journal of Palestine Studies?*

182. Where can I find articles on the 1988 Calgary Olympic Arts Festival?

183. Who publishes the periodical *Management Review* and how much does a subscription cost?

184. Where would you find a reference to an interview with Billy Joel?

185. A few months back I read a magazine in my doctor's office. It was a geology magazine, called *Earth Review* or *Earth Science Review*. Can you help me find out what the name is and where I could write to the publisher to subscribe?

186. Where can I find articles on drugs and musicians?

187. I need about a dozen sources of information on the causes of AIDS. Where do I look?

188. Where would I find listings of reviews of Barbara Taylor's *The Animal Atlas*?

189. What magazines are currently published that have to do with travel?

190. Where would you find current citations to newspapers, journals and magazines on the latest Apple computer?

191.   Is there a magazine for Sherlock Holmes aficionados? Where
        do I write to subscribe?

Reference Materials

Academic Index
Access
Agence France Press English Wire
American Newspapers, 1821-1936
AP News
Audio Video Digest
Bibliographie der fremdsprachigen Zeitschriften-Literatur
Book Review Digest
Book Review Index
Books in Series
Children's Book Review Index
Current Book Review Citations
Directory of Electronic Journals, Newsletters, and Academic
        Discussion Lists
Editor and Publisher. International Yearbook
Eventline
Foreign Broadcast Information Service
Gale Directory of Publications
Gale International Directory of Publications
History and Bibliography of American Newspapers, 1690-1820
Info Trac Videodisc
Infotrac
International Index to Multi-Media Information
International Yearbook
Internationale Bibliographie der Zeitschriftenliteratur aus allen
        Gebieten des Wissens
Irregular Serials and Annals
Magazine ASAP
Magazine Index
Magazine Industry Market Place
Media Review Digest
National Newspaper Index
NDEX

CHAPTER 9

DIRECTORIES

Reference Interviews

Patron #1.   A high school teacher.

Patron: I would like some information on SIECUS.
Librarian: Do you know what those letters stand for?
Patron: Not exactly. It has something to do with sex.
Librarian: First I'll have to look up the meaning of the letters.
               (Found in DeSola, *Abbreviations Dictionary* .) It means
               Sex Information and Education Council of the U.S.

               Where would you go for further information?

Reference Questions

1. What railroads serve Romeo, Illinois?

2. What are some of the activities of the Huguenot Historical
   Society in the U.S.?

3. Where would you look to find out if your neighbor owns his or
   her home or is renting it?

4. How many professors are on the Faculty of Theology at
   Oxford?

5. What airlines serve Tulsa, Oklahoma?

6.   Where could you find the address of the British Council in Jordan?

7.   What are the major libraries of Costa Rica?

8.   Where would you look to determine what resort establishments the American Hotel and Motel Association sponsors in Bermuda?

9.   What is the name of an airport near Pisa, Italy and which airlines use its facilities?

10.   When was the University of Cairo founded?

11.   What is the airline mileage between New York and San Francisco?

12.   Where can I locate a list of the manufacturers of steel abrasives?

13.   Are there any organizations in New Jersey which focus on ethnic folklore?

14.   What are the hours of the Metropolitan Museum of Art?

15.   Where should I look to discover what national, nonprofit associations are centered in Arkansas?

16.   Can you find a list of historical societies in the U.S.?

17.   When and where is the annual convention of the Sigmund Freud archivists usually held?

18.   What is the name of an international student relief organization and what activities does it sponsor?

19.   Find a list of dealers in foreign books.

20.   Who are the editors of Stackpole Book Publishing Company?

21.   Find a list of media available from Gaylord Bros., Inc.

22. What is the address of the National Audio Visual Center in Washington, D.C.?

23. Find a list of book clubs in the U.S.

24. Locate a calendar of media events and sponsors for the year.

25. What is the name of the general sales manager for WABC-AM radio station?

26. What is the telephone number of the Pennsylvania College of Optometry?

27. Does the Canadian Psychological Association have any publications?

28. Locate a list of universities and colleges in the Mongolian People's Republic.

29. When was Mu Phi Epsilon founded? Name some of its committees and publications.

30. When was the Rockefeller Family Fund incorporated?

31. Who was the donor of the Coleman Charitable Trust located in Kansas?

32. What is the purpose of the Metropolitan Foundation of Atlanta, Georgia?

33. Where is the Starr Foundation located?

34. Locate financial data about the Merrill Foundation.

35. Where is the National Cash Register Foundation located and what are its functions?

36. What associations are headquartered in Dearborn, Michigan?

37. How many local chapters does the Federal Bar Association have?

38. Where is the American Antiquarian Society located?

39. What is the name of the director of the Art Gallery of Hamilton, Ontario?

40. What is the address of the Lingerie Manufacturers Association?

41. When was Hiroshima University founded and how many students now attend classes?

42. Locate a list of museums in Moscow.

43. Locate a list of the members of the U.S. National Academy of Sciences.

44. What language is used for instruction at the University of Bombay, India?

45. What are the main subject collections of the Ghana National Museum?

46. Does Acheson Colloids Corporation solicit overseas trade?

47. What is the capital rating of the Western Supplies Company?

48. Where are the branch offices of the Allis-Chalmers Manufacturing Company located?

49. Who is the governing authority of the Historic Pensacola Preservation Board, located in Florida?

50. Who uses the Pensco trademark?

51. Has the Iolani Palace in Honolulu been designated an historic site?

52. Locate a list of U.S. libraries which house collections of special non-book materials.

53. How many wax museums are there in the U.S. and where are they located?

54.   Which credit cards will Japan Air Lines accept?

55.   Find a map showing the routes flown by Mexicana Airlines.

56.   What is the Pan Am airfare between New York and London?

57.   Which factories in Michigan manufacture hydraulic couplings?

58.   What is the airline fare between Detroit and Acapulco?

59.   With which institution is the Museo de Arte Religioso, located in San German, Puerto Rico, affiliated?

60.   What is the address of the American Theological Library Association?

61.   Where is the Germantown Historical Society located?

62.   What is the address of The Bookbinder's Guild of New York?

63.   What are some of the publications of the Arkansas Agricultural Experiment Station?

64.   Who is the director of the Tennessee State Museum?

65.   What special printing services does Musigraph, Inc. offer?

66.   Does Rizzoli International Publications, Inc., located in New York, have any subsidiaries?

67.   Does anyone make fluorescent light fixtures in Boston?

68.   Find a list of literary contests.

69.   Find a list of museums in London.

70.   Find a list of academies and learned societies, with descriptions, arranged by country.

71.   Find a list of book publishers who specialize in atlases and maps.

72. Locate a list of Avis and Hertz car rental agencies.

73. What is the name of a large manufacturer of greeting cards which is located in Cleveland?

74. In what state is the Acadia National Park Bookstore located?

75. Locate information on the Society for the Prevention of Cruelty to Animals.

76. What are the hours when the Mark Twain Museum in Hannibal, Missouri is open to the public?

77. What is the purpose of the National Council of Teachers of Mathematics?

78. When was the Stevens Institute of Technology in Hoboken, New Jersey founded?

79. What is the address of the company which produces Timex watches?

80. Is Allis Chalmers connected with General Motors?

81. What is the address of a company from which a patron may purchase silicone?

82. Where is the headquarters of the Cokesbury Book Shop in Syracuse, New York located?

83. What is the address of the White Sewing Machine Company?

84. The Rockwood Museum Shop in Wilmington, Delaware specializes in books on which subjects?

85. What is the address of the Benjamin Electrical Company?

86. What firms manufacture rubber suction cups?

87. Does the B. Dalton Bookseller chain have a branch store in Fargo, North Dakota?

88.   What is the address of the Corning Glass Company?

89.   What is the address of the U.S. office of the World Union of Jewish Students?

90.   Find the title of a video recording about the life cycle of the silk moth.

91.   Find the title of a film dealing with teenage sexuality.

92.   What are the titles of some filmstrips available on black studies?

93.   What information can be found in the ADELE data bases?

94.   To which publishers is the ISBN 0-8143 assigned?

95.   What is the telephone number of the National Association of Chewing Gum Manufacturers?

96.   Where is Robert Cohen, a mathematician, employed?

97.   Locate at least one title of a periodical for a reader interested in publishing an article on game theory.

98.   Find the title of a directory for municipal officials in Kansas.

99.   What is the correct name for the Better Business Bureau for the Miami area?

100.   Can you help me find the address of the Beethoven archive in Bonn, Germany?

101.   My family will be traveling to the Southwest over the summer. Where would I look to find a list of museums in that part of the country?

102.   Who is the chair of the English Department at the University of Houston?

103. I'd like a listing of names and addresses of all the museums in Detroit that specifically deal with Afro-American studies.

104. What are the areas of special interest of the antiquarian book shop in Royal Oak, Michigan?

105. What are the summer open hours and admission prices for the Museum of Science and Industry in Chicago, Illinois?

106. Where is the nearest place to obtain vegetable oil filters?

107. What films are available about the native peoples of New Zealand?

108. I've written a book about dog training and I want names and addresses of publishers and agents I can send it to.

109 . What are the research areas, collections and facilities of the San Miguel Historical Society Museum in Telluride, Colorado?

110. What is the name and address of a library association or organization in Pakistan?

111. Where can I find a list of black-owned businesses?

112. I am researching my family tree. My grandfather was Polish, and I am wondering if there's some organization devoted to Polish genealogy.

113. I'm going to Stuttgart. Do they have a university, and if so, what kinds of departments does it have? I want to take a really good history class.

114. I am doing some research in wildlife rehabilitation, and I would like to visit all of the nature centers and wildlife refuges in the state of Michigan. Where are they located?

115. I heard that an old friend of mine is one of the head honchos over at OSHA in the Department of Labor. Can you help me find her phone number?

116.   We are planning a trip to New Orleans and I would like the address and telephone number of the children's bookstore in the new Visa commercial. I think it has the word "street" in the name.

117.   How many books were published by Little, Brown & Co. in 1991?

118.   Which American libraries possess African-American collections?

119.   I want to get my short stories published, but someone said I need an agent. How do I do this?

120.   Where does Professor Anne Smith, my old home economics teacher, teach now?

121.   How many databases about astronomy are there, and who produces them?

122.   I need the address and phone/fax numbers of the University of Haifa, as well as the number of teachers/students and the name of the professor heading the Biblical Studies Department.

123.   I know there's a Fish and Game, or Wildlife and Parks, or Fish and Wildlife Library, something like that, here in Ann Arbor. It sounds like a neat place to work. Do you know if there are other branches elsewhere in the country? Because I'd rather live in the Midwest, say Nebraska or Kansas.

124.   Where can I find an up-to-date listing of information sources on computers?

125.   What is the address of the Near East Archaeological Society?

126.   What is the address for the Macmillan Publishing Company in Canada?

127.   Where can I go to find out how many students attend New York University and the number of volumes in the University's library?

128.   I need a list of Sherlock Holmes societies.

129.   How frequently is *For Your Eyes Only* updated?

130.   I need to find out what radio and T.V. stations in Birmingham, Alabama have programming aimed at the Black community.

131.   How much does it cost to advertise in the Logansport Pharos - Tribune?

132.   Where can I find the address of the NAACP?

133.   Which companies publish books on Women's Studies?

134.   Where can I find out about what national foundations or organizations are in operation for African Americans?

135.   What is the address of the Gold Prospectors Association of America?

136.   I want to write a letter to my undergraduate literature professor, Dr. W. Ralph Johnson, but he's left the university. How can I find out where he's teaching now?

Reference Materials

American Book Trade Directory
Annuaire des Organisations Internationales. Yearbook of International
        Organizations
Audio Visual Market Place
The Black Americans Information Directory
City Directories
Consumer Protection Directory
Database Directory
Directories in Print
Directory Information Service
Directory of Directories
Directory of Online Databases
Directory of Post Offices
Directory of Publishing Opportunities

168

Educational Film Locator of the Consortium of University Film Centers
Encyclopedia of Associations
The Foundation Directory
Hotel and Motel Red Book
Information Industry Market Place
Information Resources of the U.S. Government
The Literary Market Place
Museums of the World
National Faculty Directory
National Information Center for Educational Media
National Trade and Professional Associations of the United States
OAG Electronic Edition.   Travel Service
Official Airline Guide
Official Congressional Directory
Official Guide of the Railways
Official Museum Directory
Publishers' International Directory
Research Centers Directory
The Software Encyclopedia
Subject Guide to Periodical Indexes and Review Indexes
Thomas' Register of American Manufacturers
The Video Annual
The Video Source Book
World of Learning
Yearbook of International Organizations
Zip Code Directory

CHAPTER 10

GOVERNMENT PUBLICATIONS

Reference Interviews

Patron #1.   A woman.

Patron: What is the most recent address of the Social Security
                Office?
Librarian: The main office in Baltimore or a more local one?
Patron: The one in Baltimore.

                Where would you look?

Reference Questions

1. Is the journal of Rudolph F. Kurz to be found in the
    Congressional Edition? Where was it originally published in
    1937?

2. Who is the congressman for the fifth district of Minnesota in the
    present Congress?

3. An article by Rex Beach titled "Modern Miracle Men" was
    published in the Congressional Set in 1936. Where had it been
    previously printed?

4. Who are the senators and representatives from Oklahoma?

5. Where can one find a list of subjects covered in the *Subject
    Bibliographies* of government publications?

6.   Which congresspeople are on the Rules Committee?

7.   I want a list of the public documents of the Seventy-sixth
      Congress (1939-40) regarding natural resources.

8.   Who is the Chief of Naval Operations?

9.   Where would I find a list of publications by the Public Health
      Service in December of last year?

10.   What publications can be ordered from the U.S. Superintendent
      of Documents about the pulp and paper industry?

11.   Find the remarks made in the House of Representatives by
      Philip J. Philbin, Representative from Massachusetts on
      Wednesday, September 23, 1970.

12.   Locate the titles of several publications issued by NASA's
      Office of University Affairs in 1977.

13.   Where can an 1882 government report be found on the effects
      of Canadian and American tariffs?

14.   Who are the members of the House of Representatives Ways
      and Means Committee?

15.   Where can one find recent listings of the Fish and Wildlife
      Service's publications?

16.   A special report on the ship industry of the U.S. was written in
      1892. It appeared in which government document, and who
      wrote it?

17.   What report did William E. Paulson write for the U.S.
      government in 1939?

18.   Where can I find a map of the Capitol building in Washington,
      D.C.?

19.   What material was available from the Department of
      Agriculture on truck gardening in 1939?

20. Where would you go to compile a list of the publications of the State of Indiana received at the Library of Congress last year?

21. Where could I find a description of the activities of the Department of Commerce?

22. What newspapers are represented in the press galleries of the Congress?

23. Were there any government publications on defense proceedings in 1917?

24. Where can I find the voting statistics from the last Congressional election?

25. Who is the postmaster general?

26. Find a list of government publications about railroad employees.

27. Find a description of how a bill becomes a law.

28. Locate brief descriptions of the legislative histories of public laws enacted last year.

29. What are the publications of the House Ways and Means Committee?

30. Locate histories of bills concerning the spillage of oil on the U.S. coastlines.

31. What bills has your congressperson introduced during the past year?

32. Find the text of the latest debates in the Congress on bills concerning water pollution.

33. Locate the texts of the president's addresses to the Congress for last year.

34. Find a list of special publications by the House and Senate.

35. What are the contents of the Madison Papers?

36. Who wrote the report on the Piute Indians which was published in 1872?

37. On what date was W.H. Scribner awarded a disability pension by Congress for injuries received in the Civil War?

38. Who was the Senate Republican Conference Chairman of the 97th Congress?

39. What is meant by a "clean bill"?

40. Who wrote a U.S. government report in 1883 about the financial and agricultural condition of Cuba?

41. What topics did President George Washington discuss in his annual message to Congress in 1790?

42. In which volume for a given session of Congress is Senate Report #792 located?

43. Locate a list of recent state publications on art exhibitions.

44. Which title of the *Code of Federal Regulations* deals with the Census Bureau?

45. Find an organizational breakdown of the Treasury Department in chart form.

46. What became of the War Assets Administration?

47. Locate a list of Senate committees and their members.

48. In what congressional district is Washtenaw County, Michigan?

49. How is the Smithsonian Institution organized?

50. In what U.S. government document may one find a bibliography on the Eskimo language published in 1887?

51. What did the U.S. Children's Bureau publish in 1922?

52. Where can one find a brief abstract of a U.S. government report about the construction of a lighthouse at Thunder Bay, Michigan, in 1878?

53. What is the mailing address for the U.S. Department of Defense?

54. What is the best source for titles of U.S. government publications on Israel for last year?

55. Find a reference to an 1892 government report on trade relations with Mexico.

56. Find the names of the present officers of the U.S. Senate.

57. Which government agency compiled a deficiency estimate for the U.S. Geological Survey for 1892-1893?

58. Did the U.S. government publish anything on the subject of antigens and antibodies in 1939?

59. What is the serial number of the recommendation concerning the Michigan and Mississippi River Canal introduced into the House of Representatives in 1884?

60. Which radio and television correspondents are admitted to the U.S. Congressional galleries?

61. Find the name of an official report on the exploration of the Yukon River in the Alaska Territory published by the U.S. government in April, 1871.

62. Find a brief biography of Rose Long, a U.S. senator in the 1930s.

63. What is the House Document No. 381 of the 87th Congress, 2nd Session?

64. Who is the U.S. representative for the third district of this state?

65.   Are there more lawyers than representatives of any other profession in Congress?

66.   What is the address of a senator from New Jersey?

67.   Who is the chair of the National Endowment for the Humanities?

68.   Find a history of the Interstate Commerce Commission.

69.   Who is the U.S. Ambassador to the USSR?

70.   What is the formal title of the Warren Commission report?

71.   What are some of the major publications available for sale from the U.S. Government on the subject of agriculture?

72.   Where can I find the text of that heated debate on health care that the Senate had last week?

73.   On what committees does Senator Hatch serve in the Senate?

74.   What is the address of the Environmental Protection Agency?

75.   What senators are members of the standing Committee on Agriculture, Nutrition and Forestry?

76.   When was the Copyright Royalty Tribunal established and what is its function?

77.   I want to see if any of the current Congress representatives are alumni of my high school; where can I find this information?

78.   What does the U.S. government currently publish concerning library education?

79.   I want a list, with telephone numbers, of all the Government Printing Office Bookstores in the U.S.

80.   What publications, if any, are available from the U.S. Bureau of Indian Affairs?

81.   How does one become Librarian of Congress?

82.   Where can I find text of the Senate debate on Adult Immunization Awareness week?

83.   Where can I find a floor plan of the U.S. Capitol Building?

84.   I want to contact the director of the Selective Service System. Where would I find a name and address?

85.   I'm planning a trip to Washington, DC with my family. We will be doing some sightseeing. Where can I find a floor plan of the Capitol building?

86.   My professor told me to find that new Department of Health and Human Services report about aging. Please tell me where it is.

87.   How many U.S. ambassadors are women and in what countries are they serving?

88.   Where would I find a list of federal penal and correctional institutions?

89.   What are the names and party affiliations of the members of the Senate Special Committee on Aging?

90.   Who sits on either side of the vice president in the Senate chamber?

91.   What is the stated purpose of the National Aeronautics and Space Administration, and who is the current administrator?

92.   I want some information about the EEOC, including the address, phone number, activities it's involved in, and a listing of field offices/directors.

93.   When was Lowell P. Weicker, the present governor for the State of Connecticut, first elected to the U.S. Senate?

94.   What is the phone number of the nearest F.B.I. office?

95.   Where can you find the Commissioner of the Department of the
      Internal Revenue Service and his address?

96.   Where can I go to find a debate on the North American Free -
      Trade Agreement?

97.   I'd like to know what Senator Riegle has to say on a national
      policy for health care.

98.   What prayer did the Chaplain of the Senate give Oct. 7, 1992?

99.   How can I order an aeronautical chart of Alaska?

100. Who are my senators, which committees do they serve on, and
      what are their addresses?

101. How many bills became laws in the U.S. on April 21st, 1992?

102. I need a quick overview—and if possible an organizational
      chart—of what section does what in the Department of Energy.

Reference Materials

Addresses, Phone and FAX Numbers (U.S. Govt., etc.)
Biographical Directory of the American Congress
Catalogue of the Public Documents of Congress and of All
        Departments of the Government of the U.S.
Comprehensive Index to the Publications of the U.S. Government,
        1881-1893
Congressional Contact Information
Congressional Information Service Index to Publications of the U.S.
        Congress
Congressional Quarterly
Congressional Quarterly Almanac
Congressional Record
Congressional Record Abstracts

Descriptive Catalogue of the Government Publications of the U.S.
    (1774-1881)
Federal News Service
Federal Research in Progress
GPO Publications Reference File
Guide to U.S. Government Publications
Index to U.S. Government Programs
Monthly Checklist of State Publications
Monthly Catalog
Monthly Catalog of U.S. Government Publications
Monthly Checklist of State Publications
Numerical Lists and Schedule of Volumes
Official Congressional Directory
Subject Bibliographies
U.S. Government Manual

ABOUT THE AUTHOR

THOMAS P. SLAVENS (A.B., Phillips University; A.M., University of Minnesota; Ph.D. University of Michigan) is a Professor of Information and Library Studies at the University of Michigan. A former librarian at Drake University, he has taught at the University of Minnesota and the University College of Wales. He has served as president of the Association for Library and Information Science Education. Listed in *Who's Who in the World, Who's Who in America, Who's Who in American Education,* and *Contemporary Authors*, he was the first recipient of the Warner G. Rice Faculty Award at the University of Michigan and has received grants and fellowships from the Lilly Drug Co., the H.W. Wilson co., the U.S. government, and the state of Michigan. The author of twenty-four books and fifty articles in journals, he, with his wife, Cora, who is a librarian, has visited thirty countries.